REGRET-
FREE
LIVING

HOW TO FIND THE INTERSECTION
OF YOUR PASSIONS AND GIFTEDNESS

SCOT SELLERS

ENDORSEMENTS

"*Regret-Free Living* is a wonderful guide for the young—and not so young—to use as you think about a better definition of the good life. In sharing his career and personal journey, Scot Sellers gives practical examples, and challenges us to first discover our gifts and passions, and then to put them to use in a life-giving way for ourselves and our communities."

Jonathan Reckford
Chief Executive Officer, Habitat for Humanity

"Scot Sellers' new book, *Regret-Free Living*, is a must-read for those who are seeking a peaceful and accomplished life. It is filled with meaningful stories and practical suggestions we can all find beneficial. I LOVE this book!"

David Martin
Former Chairman and
CEO, Young Presidents' Organization

"Scot Sellers, in *Regret-Free Living*, emphasizes the importance of creating a worthy mission to produce sustainable success in one's professional and personal life. Readers are encouraged to engage in continuous and candid self-appraisal in order to find the intersection of their personal passions and skill sets. The book also emphasizes the need for self-improvement and taking prudent risks, recognizing that criticism and potential failure may be companions in that effort. The author's advice is analogous to Stoic philosophy—a life well lived is more important than conventional definitions of success. Sellers provides reminders (and confirmation) for good leaders and invaluable advice to those striving to become good leaders."

Jim Hackett
Former Chairman/CEO, Anadarko Petroleum,
Partner, Riverstone Holdings LLC,
Former Chairman of the Federal Reserve Bank of Dallas

"Scot Sellers, in his *Regret-Free Living*, has distilled valuable lessons from his years in leadership to create a primer on living and leading without regrets. He combines a strong message and easy-to-implement next steps with readable personal stories. I highly recommend this book to all business executives, especially those in the next generation."

Mac McQuiston

Chairman/Founder CEO, Forum

Published in Boise, Idaho by Elevate Publishing.
A division of Elevate Publishing.

For more information please visit www.elevatepub.com
or email us at info@elevatepub.com.

Editorial Work: AnnaMarie McHargue
Cover Design: Arthur Cherry
Interior Design: Aaron Snethen

Paperback ISBN-13: 9781945449109
eBook ISBN-13: 9781945449116

The events mentioned in this book are actual events, but in many cases the names have been changed to retain the anonymity of those involved.

For the sake of simplicity, the author has chosen to use the masculine pronoun "him" when referring to an unnamed individual.

TABLE OF CONTENTS

This book is dedicated to my loving family. To my mom and dad, Walt and Diolenda Sellers, who always loved and supported me. To my beautiful wife and best friend, Keely, who is my partner in everything. To my five wonderful children, Danielle, Ross, Bri, Kaitlyn, and Alyssa—you make life fun and rewarding.

REGRET-FREE LIVING

HOW TO FIND THE INTERSECTION
OF YOUR PASSIONS AND GIFTEDNESS

INTRODUCTION

I was 14 years old, a sophomore at a large (nearly 4,000 students) high school in Southern California, and desperate to fit in with the popular crowd. Being young for my grade, and small (five-foot-three and 105 pounds), made fitting in even more difficult.

Fortunately, in Spanish class I sat behind Debbie, who was one of the popular girls, and she enjoyed talking with me. Early that school year, she made sure I was included in one of the first birthday parties of the season, at the home of one of the popular girls. I couldn't believe it when the invitation came in the mail! It was my chance to make friends with all of the kids I longed to sit with during lunch, to hang out with between classes, and to go to after school activities with. The three weeks until the party couldn't pass quickly enough.

That Saturday finally came, and although I had to endure the indignity of my mom driving me to the party (nearly all of the kids going to the party had their own cars, as it was mostly juniors and seniors in attendance), I walked up to the door and rang the doorbell. One of the blonde-haired beauties I had admired from afar opened the door, greeted me with a smile, and invited me in. The house was almost as beautiful as she was, and I immediately noticed many of the star athletes from our school out in the backyard, shirts off, swim trunks on, enjoying the sun.

The invitation said there would be a pool, but I didn't bring my swim trunks. Being slow to start puberty and young for my grade made the thought of going shirtless in front of a group of my peers terrifying. Plus, because I was slightly overweight and lacked any sort of muscle definition, I had already decided that I would use the excuse that I was recovering from a cold to avoid swimming at the party.

The first hour of the party was awkward as I tried to join a few of the conversations going on around the pool. While I did my best to be interesting, it seemed the more I tried, the more out of place I felt. I was relieved when Debbie finally arrived at the party, and I made my way over to talk to her. She was very nice to me, and introduced me to several of her friends. The next half hour was a bit more comfortable for me as I listened to what others in the group were saying, and tried to act like I belonged, even while feeling out of place inside.

I was in a small group, with my back to the pool, when I noticed one of the biggest football players standing next to me, smiling. He introduced himself, and then he and his friend picked me up, carried me over to the pool, and tossed me in, fully clothed.

The humiliation of being thrown into the swimming pool while wearing your best *cool* party clothes, in front of more than 100 of the most popular kids in your high school, is indescribable. Let's just say it wasn't my best day.

Although I wanted to cry, I held back my tears and tried to laugh, and thanked the guys for showing me the pool. Everyone laughed and clapped as I swam to the edge and climbed out, dripping wet, then nearly fell in again in while fishing out my shoe that had come off.

Fortunately, the hostess' mom noticed the commotion and brought a towel over for me, then walked me into the house, still dripping wet. I didn't have a change of clothes, and really didn't want to go back outside to face more ridicule, so I called my mom and asked her to pick me up, telling her I had fallen into the pool.

I spent the rest of the weekend reflecting on what happened to me, thinking about why they picked me out of the group, why none of the kids came inside to check on me, or even say goodbye to me when I left. The answer was relatively easy, but hard to admit—I didn't really belong in that group of kids. I was trying to fit into a place that I wasn't ready for at that time. Somehow, even though I tried to act like I belonged there, everyone else could tell that I didn't. The thought of that revelation left me cold, but I knew it was accurate.

I didn't want to be relegated to social obscurity, but I also didn't want to invite further humiliation, so that weekend I made the decision that I was going to study life thoroughly and carefully. I wanted to understand how relationships work and to figure out what brings happiness and fulfillment to people. Perhaps even more importantly, I wanted to understand myself more fully and discover how I fit into all of this.

My new resolve and focus didn't mean that I no longer experienced awkward moments during my developmental years. In fact, I still had many more embarrassing and humiliating moments. However, during my sophomore year, I did find a group of friends that I enjoyed spending time with, which was a great solace for me as I struggled to understand myself, and how I would fit into the world around me.

My small group of friends was a great source of belonging for me until, at the end of my sophomore year in high school, my family decided to move from suburban Orange County, California, to a small, rural town in southern Oregon. So, I began my junior year in a tiny, backward southern

Oregon town, where I had to adapt to a completely different culture—a small high school, whose students had little interest in academics or college, and a big focus on muscle sports (which left me out), and logging. I didn't fit into this culture at all (and decided that I didn't want to try), which allowed me time to work hard and save money for college. I also got my first job managing a business, and even though it was a small, company-owned service station, it taught me a lot. I learned that being a dependable employee makes you incredibly valuable, and that developing an attitude of respect and service to others, leads to opportunities for increased responsibilities and advancement.

Despite my ambivalence to high school social life, I did well in my academics and earned a lot of financial assistance for my college years at Lewis and Clark College in Portland, Oregon. College was a time of tremendous discovery for me, especially as I learned more about myself, and the *art* of nurturing relationships with others. I have devoted significant effort, during the 42 plus years since starting college, to a careful study of life and relationships. The key lessons learned along the way have made my life incredibly enjoyable and rewarding. The goal of this book is to share the results of my insights and introspection with you, in order that these "life lessons" may enhance your life's journey.

For a quick "fast forward" from my college experience, in less than 19 years I found myself promoted to be the CEO of a large, publicly traded real estate company, and had the good fortune to lead this company for over 20 great, fun-filled years. In this role, I was very fortunate to be able to spend a lot of time with highly motivated and extremely successful people. What I discovered was that many of them were very singularly focused (usually around their business careers), and often seemed to miss the other components of life that bring real joy and lasting fulfillment.

If you ask a group of successful people the question, "Outside of your career and your family, what is your passion?" many will tell you that they don't know. Or, for those who do know, they have precious little time to pursue this passion. Our lives are meant to be passionate. They are intended to be full of adventure, and rewarding in many ways, including your career.

None of us wants to get to the end of our life, only to look back with regret on the many things we missed. The best way to avoid that, and to take advantage of all that life has to offer, is to learn all you can about yourself, and about how you fit in with the tremendous opportunities that surround you. The more you seek wisdom, the more you will find that continuous exploration will help you maximize all aspects of your life.

May you enjoy your journey!

PREFACE

I have enjoyed a very interesting journey to date, and am looking forward to many more adventures in a life filled with passion and loving relationships. The life lessons in the following chapters come from my experiences in school, sports, life, and business.

I was fortunate to serve, for many years, as the Chairman and CEO of what ultimately became a large, publicly traded real estate company called, Archstone. Many of my life lessons on leadership, culture, and values came from my time there, as I had the opportunity to work with an incredible number of talented and committed colleagues.

My initial intention in writing this book was to share a compendium of lessons learned, overlaid with the progression of my life and career, but it became challenging to conform everything to a strict chronology and still appropriately cover each topic. As a result, the lessons learned sometimes cross over different segments of my life's journey and chronology, but are hopefully organized in a relevant manner. It is my hope that the mixture of lessons from different aspects of life will provide a more useful understanding of the issues at hand, while the personal anecdotes provide interest and context.

The blessing of our life is that if we never stop learning, we never stop growing.

The blessing of our life is that if we never stop learning, we never stop growing.

Chapter 1
Discovering Your Giftedness

Life is an adventure, and, fortunately, one that provides an environment for continuous learning. From the time we are born, we learn at a tremendous pace. We learn languages, tastes, sounds, dangers, pleasures, and so much more. We learn about the world around us, and we learn about ourselves.

Devoted parents begin teaching their children sounds and colors, well before they start school, and learning continues at a rapid pace as we advance through our schooling. In high school and college, we learn much more about social systems and dynamics, and begin to prepare for independence from our parents. Some of us continue in school, beyond college, to pursue advanced degrees, and some continue further still, doing post-doctoral research.

Interestingly, the majority of this process is focused on learning facts, behaviors, and skills related to our external environment. Very little of this learning is intentionally directed at learning about ourselves, and the unique characteristics we each possess.

Although American culture celebrates and encourages individualism and inventiveness much more than nearly any other nation in the world, our school system still primarily emphasizes a specific type of academic achievement. This educational emphasis is primarily focused on the ability to memorize and retain certain essential facts, and to provide this information when queried for regular exams. Students who are gifted in areas that differ from our primary educational system sometimes find themselves feeling unsuccessful and left out, even though they have tremendously valuable skills to offer.

The important thing to remember is that each of us has particular gifts in different areas of life. One of the most important areas of learning we can pursue—as early as possible in our lives—is to discover our own unique areas of "giftedness." As we discover this giftedness, we can then work to develop the capabilities we are most naturally blessed with.

It is also helpful to understand those areas in which we are not particularly gifted. This doesn't mean that we shouldn't pursue those particular activities or disciplines, especially if we have a strong passion for them, but it helps to provide us with a realistic assessment of how much we might be able to achieve in a given area, relative to the efforts we invest in it.

My first experience with understanding the concept of giftedness occurred in the same sophomore year of high school mentioned earlier. As already noted, nobody in my high school would have described me as particularly athletic, but I decided to work hard at making the high school golf team. I had been taking lessons and practicing diligently since eighth grade, and felt that if I worked hard enough in high school, I could make the team. I practiced on the driving range from one to three hours each weekday, and played nine or 18 holes of golf as often as I could afford to on the weekends.

My freshman year of high school provided a great platform to improve my game. Every day after school, anyone going out for the golf team was allowed free practice time on the range at our home course, as well as free tee times after 3 p.m. From that time on, we could play as many holes as we could get in before dark. Nearly every weekday evening my mom would faithfully drive to the course to pick me up, about 30 minutes after sunset, being very supportive of my efforts to ultimately earn the right to make the team.

There were typically six people who played for our school team in each match, and I wasn't quite good enough to make the team as a freshman. My scores improved throughout the year, and by the end of my freshman year, I was scoring in the low 80s (which I felt pretty good about). However, I still needed to get my score down another four or five strokes in order to make our team (which as any avid golfer knows, is a very tall order). I continued to work hard over the summer to achieve this goal.

When practice began during my sophomore year, I noticed that we had a couple of new freshman trying out for the team, and our coach asked me to go out and play nine holes with the two of them. They were both small in stature, about my size, and very nice guys. However, after a few holes, the difference in giftedness between one of them, and me, was astounding.

This freshman golfer, only 15 years old, was two strokes under par after six holes, and had a seemingly effortless swing. Like me, he couldn't hit the ball much more than 180 to 200 yards off the tee, but his short game was remarkable. He just had a feel for the golf clubs and how to impart spin on the ball that I couldn't achieve, no matter how much I played.

That was my first exposure to giftedness in the athletic world. I still worked out with the team every day of the year, but I never got good enough to make the competitive team. With the arrival of those new players, the bar to make the team was raised substantially, as three of the six members of our high school team routinely shot under par rounds—an enormous gap from my occasional high 70s round! It is worth noting that the freshman golfer mentioned here was Mark

O'Meara, who went on to win many professional titles, including the US Open.

Despite the fact that I am not gifted at golf, I have continued to play the sport throughout my life, and have even recorded one or two sub-par rounds (but not with any regularity). I really enjoy golf as a way to relax, build relationships, and participate in good, old-fashioned camaraderie and competition. However, the reality is that no matter how much I practice, I don't have the giftedness at golf to earn a living as a golfer. The importance of understanding this, early in my life, was that I could pursue my enjoyment of golf as a fun hobby, but not frustrate myself by trying to earn a living in an area that is not my strength. Instead, I chose to pursue other areas of my life to identify my true giftedness.

The process of discovering your giftedness requires trying a number of different things, most of which will be unfamiliar when you make your first attempt. As you gain the courage to undertake new endeavors, you may be shocked at the skills and capabilities you uncover.

For instance, who would have thought that the kid thrown in the pool by the popular kids in high school would have the gift of leadership? As I moved through high school and into college, a leadership position was the last thing I had in mind for my future. I saw my giftedness as being in math, science, and intellectual pursuits, probably leading to more of a "back of the house" kind of a career.

What began to change this was my willingness to try some new things, combined with feedback from others around me. Obtaining thoughtful feedback from others is another essential component to discovering your giftedness. It is often extremely difficult, if not impossible, to perceive ourselves as others see us.

In my freshman year of college, three of the guys in my dorm had met Ron, an alumnus who was trying to re-establish the fraternity he had belonged to when he attended school there. Because it had disbanded, Ron was trying to recruit leaders at our small college who would be able to restart the Sigma Alpha Epsilon (SAE) chapter from scratch—on a campus that had no real fraternities.

He had identified three big, athletic guys who all happened to live in my dorm (they all looked very much like the prototype of a leader to me—tall, handsome and playing varsity sports at our school), and somehow they had decided to approach me about joining them. They saw something in me that I didn't see at the time—the ability to gain the trust of other people. Without this insight from my peers, and my willingness to be thrust into a position of vulnerability (recruiting new people to join our fledgling fraternity), I would not have been able to begin the process of discovering that I possessed a surprising new area of giftedness—one that ultimately became my career—leadership.

This is another key prerequisite to discovering your giftedness—you must be willing to take risks, you must be willing to be embarrassed, and even to fail at new tasks. We are all generally reluctant to try new things. We don't want to look unskilled or awkward in front of others, or even worse, to fail in front of others. However, without the willingness to try new things (and even fail at times), we will confine ourselves to very narrow areas of life, and will fail to realize our full potential. We simply must convince ourselves that a critical part of our continual learning, throughout our lives, is to try our hand at new activities and challenges and, in the process, learn more about ourselves.

The process of examining the huge array of different skills and capabilities that exist inside of us, and understanding where our natural talents reside, is very fun and exceptionally rewarding. The results help us to calibrate our career path and goals, as well as determine how we spend some of our leisure time. Knowing and understanding your particular giftedness also assists you in identifying people who possess gifts that differ from your own. This is particularly benificial when building a team of people to accomplish a specific task. This is one of the most crucial elements of successful teams—having the right people in the right positions at the right time—easy to say, but challenging to do.

Keep in mind, though, that giftedness is a relative concept. The critical construct to understand is how our personal giftedness differs within our individual range of skills. An example of this is a person who is an incredible all-around athlete, and is skilled at many different sports, but even he will typically be truly gifted at only one or two sports. Remember Michael Jordan trying to earn the right to become a major league baseball player? Even though he was one of the best basketball players of all time, he was not truly gifted as a baseball player.

As you work to discover your giftedness, remember to:

1. Actively explore multiple areas of expertise, and be willing to be adventuresome in doing so. Maintain a lifelong willingness to venture well outside of your comfort zone to try new things. You will be pleasantly surprised by the results.

2. Recognize that you will naturally excel at those areas you are most gifted in. Whether this is in sports, business, arts, science, politics, or any other area of life, your areas of giftedness are those that are the most likely to produce success and fulfillment for you over the years.

3. Intentionally seek feedback from others about your particular area of skills, as well as those areas that are not perceived to be your strong suits. The feedback from a single individual isn't definitive, but as you gather feedback from a number of different people, you begin to form an effective picture of your specific giftedness.

4. Keep a continual list of your giftedness (as well as those areas that aren't your strengths), and use it to help you evaluate anything you are considering being involved in, including employment, volunteer activities, hobbies, or other leisure pursuits.

5. Never stop trying new things and never stop learning.

6. Be willing to be embarrassed and even to fail when trying new things. Find the fun in the process, and remember that learning about yourself makes you a better, more well-rounded person.

Chapter 2
Identifying Your Passions

One of my favorite questions to ask people is, "Outside of your family and your career, what are your passions?" Try the question at a social gathering sometime, or in casual conversation. You will find the results fascinating.

Over the years I have found that many executives have a very difficult time answering this question. For many of them, the reality is that the demands of career and family have made it exceptionally difficult to find time (I prefer to say make time since we all have the same number of hours in the day available to us), to pursue their passion(s), or perhaps even to remember what they are, or *were*.

A deeper conversation about passions often reveals a childhood passion, like playing the piano, for instance, that has long been forgotten with the ascendancy of career. When you get someone talking about these types of passions, there often is a longing to reconnect with that passion, because the connection is really an inextricable part of who they are.

Just as discovering your giftedness is an essential component of self-awareness (and, I believe, pivotal to ultimate success and fulfillment in life), the same is true about identifying your passions. Again, just as with giftedness, our passions span the entire gamut of life disciplines and experiences. Understanding our passions helps us make better decisions about our career pursuits, relationships, family objectives, and recreational activities.

Similar to our search for giftedness, we identify our passions by experimenting. We expose ourselves to different situations and experiences, take classes in school that are different from our core comfort zone, and try new activities that we have never tried before. Again, we need to be adventuresome, willing to fail, and perhaps even to be a bit embarrassed by our performance, or lack thereof. In the midst of this exploration, we should be constantly on the lookout for those experiences that make us feel truly alive, energized, and excited.

I coached a lot of different sports teams for my son, Ross, as he grew up. (My coaching competence was exhausted when he started eighth grade, and the game playbooks grew too sophisticated for my basic level of experience with the sports.) I could always tell the kids who were passionate about a given sport. These were the kids who didn't want practice to be over and asked if we could get together for informal practices on off days. Their passion drove them to practice on their own, with no motivation from anyone but themselves.

Ross displayed this level of passion with basketball, tennis, and lacrosse. He and I were constantly in the back yard or driveway, playing one of these three sports together, or with some of his teammates. It was great fun to see some of these passions emerge at a young age. Whenever he is home from college today, the first thing he wants to do is to play tennis with me. It is a passion we share together, even though neither of us would say that we are gifted at tennis at a level above being good recreational players.

I discovered my passion for tennis during my freshman year in college. I went out for the golf team, and I made the team (once again), but wasn't quite good enough to make the traveling team (familiar story!). Coincidentally, one of the guys who I was working on the fraternity with was a great tennis player, so I asked him if we could hit some balls together. He was kind enough to agree (since I had played very little tennis prior to that), and even though I was just learning, I fell in love with the sport. I enjoyed it so much that I played tennis for many hours each day, for the rest of my college career. With the benefit of 25+ hours of tennis each week (weather permitting), I improved enough that I was able to make our college tennis team during my sophomore year. I earned the last of the six traveling team positions and got to travel with the team. This was a dream come true for me!

I continued to play tennis for two to three hours each day after graduating from college, and my two years at Stanford Business School provided nearly unlimited time to play tennis with great players. Admittedly, I often selected time on the tennis courts instead of time in the classroom. In fact, my Stanford classmates knew me as the guy who carried three tennis rackets around in his backpack every day and who often left class early for tennis matches.

When you are passionate about something, you want to pursue it as often as you can. It brings such joy and fulfillment that it adds an incredibly positive dimension to your life that is simply missing without it.

My passion for tennis hasn't faded. In 2007, I even took time from my CEO duties at our large company to play several national tournaments in the 50 and over age category, which was incredibly fun.

Of course, it is absolutely essential to arrange your priorities appropriately, but that is a subject for another chapter.

Please don't misunderstand my emphasis here, your family and career should be among the most important passions in your life, but I firmly believe that it is important to have one or more passions, in addition to your family and your career.

Areas of passion could be virtually anything (e.g., playing an instrument, singing, traveling, playing a sport, spiritual pursuits, painting, or many others). The key is to develop a deep enough understanding of yourself so that you know and embrace your particular areas of passion.

So far, this discussion has focused primarily on passions that relate to leisure pursuits. Of course, the reality is that it is also critically important to develop a deep understanding of your passions as they relate to career and learning disciplines. A full comprehension of your passions in these areas will produce much greater career fulfillment and long-term success.

In the early years of my career, I noticed that many people worked at jobs they didn't enjoy. Even worse, they weren't working toward a future role that would energize them, but instead were just "doing their jobs." If they remained in their current roles, they were destined for a tolerable work life, but not a work life they enjoyed and were stimulated by.

I believe that our careers were meant to be enjoyable and fulfilling. If we are involved in roles we are passionate about, we are energized by our jobs and perform at a much higher level of achievement. In order to identify a position or career that provides this level of fulfillment, it is first necessary to understand your own passions.

My own journey required a few twists and turns. I already mentioned that some of my areas of giftedness were math and science. They came easily to me, and I excelled in these classes with little or no work. The natural extension of this aptitude seemed to be a career in medicine or dentistry, which is what I pursued during my first three years in college. Although I continued to excel in these classes (while still playing tennis most of the time), they didn't excite me.

I believed that once I actually got into my medical or dental career, I would enjoy it more, because I would be doing something tangible. During spring break of my junior year, a girl I was dating invited me to visit her family in the San Francisco Bay Area. Her father was an oral surgeon, and upon hearing of my interest in a career in the medical field, invited me to observe him the next morning as he performed a quadruple impaction removal. I didn't know it at the time, but suffice it to say, the process was brutal.

As soon as I saw him hammering away on a chisel to break the impacted teeth into pieces, the room got very warm and started to spin, and I had to leave—I did not, indeed, could not, return. That was all it took to help me understand that the reality of a career in the medical or dental field wasn't for me, even though my grades and test scores would allow me entrance to these coveted graduate schools. I am very thankful that I had the opportunity to learn that a medical career wasn't a fit as early in the process as I did. Without this spring break experience, I likely would have pursued this career path much longer than I should have.

After this realization, I had absolutely no idea what I wanted to do after college. I was back to square one. Fortunately, one of my friends suggested applying to graduate programs in business, because it was a broad enough field of study to allow me to find something I might be interested in.

Business school was fun, I learned a lot, and also played many hours of tennis with great players. Stanford was a real tennis mecca at that time. I landed a prime job at the Boston Consulting Group for the summer between school years, but realized that I didn't enjoy simply studying problems and then telling others how to solve them. I longed to do something tangible.

One of the blessings of the second year in the MBA program is that hundreds of employers come to campus with the hopes of hiring upcoming graduates. I took advantage of this unprecedented access and interviewed with with over 50 different companies in an effort to identify a career that fit my passions.

Fortunately, during the process, I stumbled across the real estate development industry. The development industry creates something very tangible (new buildings), requires complex problem solving skills, and is quite varied in job content. It wasn't easy to get a job in the industry in those days (the real estate recession of 1980-82 was severe and painful), but dogged persistence landed me a job with Lincoln Property Company, which, at the time, was the largest developer of apartment buildings in the country.

To be honest, I worked very hard to get a job with the Trammell Crow Company or the Gerald Hines Company, companies that built huge office skyscrapers, instead of the drab, two-story wood apartment buildings that were Lincoln Property Company's signature product. In addition, I loved the sunshine and ocean access of California, so targeted my efforts at real estate positions in either Southern or Northern California. However, despite my efforts, the only job offer I received in real estate was developing apartments with Lincoln (and in Denver, Colorado, of all places), so I accepted it, because the job content really aligned with my interests, even though the physical product wasn't what I envisioned.

I had already spent a lot of time understanding my passions and my giftedness, but I still had a long way to go in further refining that understanding. Taking this job allowed me to try many new areas of responsibility and to develop a much more comprehensive understanding of my passions and capabilities, which in turn allowed me to begin to build my career. Without the exploration I had done to date, I wouldn't have selected the right industry for myself. Knowing myself in depth facilitated a successful career choice, which is why pursuing self-discovery is so important.

When I interview potential new hires, I always ask them to describe the job tasks and types of responsibilities they are passionate about. The majority of people I interview don't really have a strong answer to that question. It takes time and purposeful self-discovery to uncover the answers to this question.

One way to evaluate job skills and responsibilities is to consider five primary areas of the workplace: (a) managing people/building teams, (b) transactional skills/negotiating/sales, (c) technological capabilities/information technology, (d) accounting/finance/back office, and (e) strategic decision making/capital allocation. A company functions best when people have positions of responsibility that require the skill sets they are passionate about, which is much easier to say than to actually accomplish. A great manager must have a strong understanding of his people in order to identify their skills and passions and help them find the positions that maximize these capabilities. This requires time, a caring spirit for people, and the ability to understand others in depth.

For example, if you want to manage people, what aspects of this position do you really love doing? If you don't truly love taking the time to develop an understanding of the hopes, dreams, and challenges of each of your direct reports, and helping them work through them, you probably aren't *that* passionate about what it takes to be a great manager.

Consider the passions required for a career in the finance area of a company. Great finance people love solving puzzles. They are generally perfectionists who derive deep satisfaction from creating order from confusion, and getting everything to fit together in its proper place. If this sort of thing is tedious for you, then pursuing a career in accounting won't align well with your passions, and trying to make it work will likely produce only limited satisfaction.

Those who are passionate about sales love meeting new people, and being thrust into new situations where they must decipher the keys to establishing a successful relationship. They are much more comfortable with rejection than most of us, and thrive on a fast-paced, high-energy environment. Success at sales requires a unique set of skills and passions, and is incredibly fulfilling for those with the passion for this area of the business world. Conversely, it is incredibly frustrating for those without the passions needed to align with this career path.

Sometimes a manager has to help those he supervises to identify their passions and align their job responsibilities accordingly. This process may involve allowing employees to try new positions where they may fail, but the results can also be tremendously exciting. An example from one of my colleagues at Archstone provides a helpful context for understanding the importance of identifying passions in the workplace.

John's work for Archstone as an analyst involved the frequent preparation of complicated spreadsheets, which analyzed key ratios at different apartment properties we owned and managed. His work product helped us to identify areas where we could improve operating efficiencies, which is very important in the apartment business. He had been with us for two years and did an excellent job, but wasn't fulfilled by his work, and was considering leaving us.

One of the managerial tools we used regularly was to sit down with our people every two years and ask them about their dreams for their future, and what they hoped to accomplish. It gave them a chance to dream a bit, and think about other jobs they might like with our company, or even away from the company. Over the years, several of our employees left to start new businesses, sometimes with our financial backing. This proved to be very rewarding for them, as well as for our management team. The practice of digging deep to better understand your employees' goals and objectives is an excellent managerial tool.

When we sat down with John, he told us that what he really dreamed of doing was becoming an acquisitions officer in our industry, which means being out in the field every day and identifying apartment properties to purchase for tens or even hundreds of millions of dollars (at this point in time we were purchasing approximately $1.5 billion in apartment properties annually). The skills required for this endeavor are very different from those needed to be a successful analyst. Instead of being in the back office preparing numerical analyses, you need to be out meeting with brokers and owners, identifying desirable properties to purchase, and then engaging in very detailed negotiations to successfully structure large, complex transactions. You also need to be very comfortable with rejection, because you get told, "no" a lot!

John's background before starting his career was in competitive athletics, and his back office position wasn't satisfying the competitive drive that he had a strong passion for. He assured us he would work harder than anyone else to become successful as an acquisition officer (and we believed him!), so we decided to give him the chance to pursue his dream, and his passion.

In just three years, John became one of the top acquisition officers in our company. He was so good at his job that he acquired a greater volume of apartment properties in his territory than any other company we competed against in the same geography. Interestingly, his income ultimately increased more than tenfold from his position as an analyst.

That is what passion can do for you when you identify the right career path. It has been over 15 years since we gave John his opportunity, and he is still a highly successful acquisitions officer in the real estate industry today.

At this point in our discussion about passions, it is important to acknowledge that pursuing your passions doesn't always produce significant financial remuneration. Sometimes our passions lead us in directions that are inconsistent with the opportunity to acquire significant material wealth. For example, a passion for serving the poor could lead you to a career in the non-profit world, working in remote overseas locations for very modest compensation. However, if this is what makes you feel truly alive and fulfilled, it would be a shame not to pursue it.

Others with a passion for serving the poor may decide to organize their careers so that this is a significant part of what they do with their time and money, while still working at a more "commercially oriented" career path. In other instances, people with this passion retire early so they can donate more of their time and money to efforts to serve others.

The notable thing about these different approaches is that all of them recognize the passion the individual has to serve the poor, and allows for this to be a meaningful part of their life. Whether it is done as a full-time job, part-time work, or subsequent to an early retirement is a very individual decision, and should not be made based on the earnings potential from the path selected. Instead, each person must identify his passions and opportunities, and then make a careful decision to allocate time and resources accordingly.

The most important message of this chapter is to take the time to learn about yourself. Learn about your areas of giftedness, and explore, explore, and explore some more to identify your passions. The more you know about what brings out feelings of pure fulfillment in you, the more you can orient your career, and life pursuits, around those areas.

Passions don't always make sense, they don't always earn money, and they aren't always easy to embrace. However, pursuing your passions brings joy and satisfaction to your life in a way that little else can.

As you spend time identifying your passions, remember to:

1) Have fun exploring different opportunities. Try things that are very different from your previous experiences, you may discover passions in the most unlikely areas.

2) Don't be afraid to be a bit uncomfortable when trying new things, everyone has a "first time" at a new endeavor. Embrace the joy of discovering new experiences and creating memories.

3) Remember that passions don't always necessarily produce monetary rewards, but the intangible rewards are of much greater value.

4) Passions help to create joy and magic in life, which, in turn, create special memories and satisfaction.

If you identify something that you are both passionate about, and gifted at, you will find yourself engaged, challenged, and satisfied with your progress and success.

Chapter 3
Finding Your Intersection

When making career decisions, pursue the areas where your passions and your giftedness intersect.

As you invest the time to learn more about yourself by discovering your areas of giftedness and passion, you come to decision points. Where do I allocate my time? What do I select as my career focus, and how do I make corrective adjustments along the way? These are the critical decisions that, made properly, will bring great satisfaction and enjoyment to your life.

If you are gifted at something, but not passionate about it, you will eventually find yourself bored and unsatisfied with your direction, and, in fact, looking for a change. By contrast, if you are passionate about something, but not gifted at it, you will be very engaged, but often frustrated that it takes more more time for you to achieve results, which then leads to your rate of progress being less satisfying.

However, if you identify something that you are both passionate about, and gifted at, you will find yourself engaged, challenged, and satisfied with your progress and success.

Further refining the understanding of your passions and giftedness is essential if you are to enjoy a fun, rewarding, and successful career. Pursuing a career that produces anything less than these benefits shortchanges yourself. And, yes, I did include FUN in the list of attributes that our careers should produce for us. Our work should be engaging, and it should be fun!

As we built our relatively small apartment company into a large, successful company called, "Archstone," one piece of advice I repeatedly gave to our associates was to "work hard, be true to our values, serve others, and have fun!" With over 3,000 associates who enjoyed their jobs, our company had an incredibly strong culture that produced continued successes, and very happy employees, customers, and stakeholders.

When our careers intersect with our passions and our giftedness, we find that success comes more easily, the work itself is rewarding, and the process is fun. Isn't that the kind of career that everyone desires?

My own journey in finding my intersection took longer than I expected. I had to try a number of different jobs in my chosen field of real estate to find the sweet spot for my particular giftedness and passions. I began my real estate career in the development of new apartment complexes, which produced a very steep learning curve.

The development process for me was interesting, as it allowed me to be something akin to a symphony conductor, selecting and coordinating a team of experts to bring everything together to produce a beautiful end-product. Some of these experts work for you directly, while others are hired contractors. Coordinating all of these disparate personalities and talents to work together requires a broad capability to manage different skill sets, egos, and motivation levels. To me, succeeding despite those challenges is what made the process so exciting.

In addition to being great conductors, outstanding real estate developers are incredibly focused on the smallest of details, in order to produce an exceptional final product. This means spending time on colors and specification requirements for everything from the largest components to the smallest—

faucets and door knobs, for example—so that every piece works together perfectly to achieve the desired end result.

I developed thousands of new apartment units in my early career, and had a great time doing so, but as I progressed in those early years, a more subtle distinction of my skill set became apparent to me. I really loved the leadership, conducting, and motivational aspect of the development process, as well as the negotiation of the deal, but the more detailed portions of the process were less interesting to me.

Over time, I realized that my true giftedness was in the leadership of others, building a cohesive team, and successfully achieving difficult goals together. My passions were for competitive achievement (some people call it winning). I also loved solving complex problems, and doing as many transactions as possible. The thrill of negotiating and producing winning results was captivating to me.

My intersection of giftedness and passions aligned much more closely with a senior leadership role in a real estate enterprise, rather than as a pure real estate developer. When I was given the opportunity to run our company, I hired talented real estate developers to work for our company—those who loved managing the smallest details to create exceptional new properties—because they were far better at this part of the process than I was. Together, as a cohesive team, we were all incredibly happy and fulfilled, and were infinitely more successful than any of us could have been on our own.

This is the way successful teams are built. The leader must understand his strengths and weaknesses, and then hire experts in those areas of weakness to build an exceptional overall enterprise. Also important, though, is the leader's willingness to allow those experts to pursue their passions and expertise, providing thoughtful guidance and continual encouragement, rather than under strict constraints, which stifle creativity.

It is by first finding your own intersection, and then helping those you work with to find their intersections, that winning teams are built. Teams are far more powerful than a collection of individuals because each member of the team makes the other members stronger than they would be on their own.

Finding your intersection may sound easy, but it often requires a lot of time and varied experiences. It took 13 years, after starting my career in real estate, for me to fully refine my understanding of my own intersection. Along the way, I'd had a number of different jobs that each contributed a small component to my overall understanding. However, it took working at these different positions to compile a complete understanding of my intersection.

My position as a developer reinforced my love of leadership, transactions, and negotiating. Running a property management company deepened my appreciation for the value of building strong, highly motivated teams, and the tremendous satisfaction derived from that. While running the "workout department" (the team that worked on restructuring loans that we were no longer able to pay due to an economic downturn) during the real estate recession of the early 1990s stimulated my competitive and intellectual side, I missed the excitement of transactions and leadership. My job as an acquisitions officer was an adrenaline rush due to the sheer volume of transactions we completed, but I missed the satisfaction that came from building and leading a large team of people.

Those 13 years of different experiences helped me to understand that my passions and giftedness intersected at a place of leadership and team building, in a fast-paced, competitive, transactional environment. We used this playbook to build

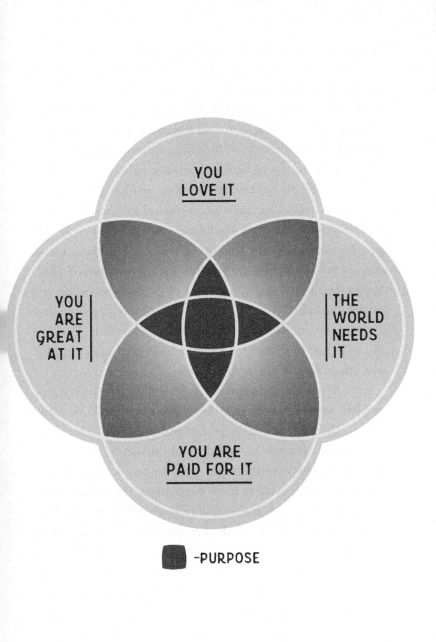

Archstone into an industry-leading company, from humble beginnings, and, in the process, all of us had more fun than we ever thought possible.

An example from the career progression of one of the young people we hired in our management development program provides another look at finding your intersection.

Jane joined our company fresh out of a well-respected MBA program, with no specific idea of what area of our company she wanted to work in. She was a former physics teacher, highly intelligent, loved solving problems, and enjoyed people. We gave her assignments in finance, operations, investments, and technology in an effort to help her identify her intersection. She evolved from her early role as a problem solver in our operations group, to become the leader of our merger integration team on the largest company purchase we ever made. It was in this role that she discovered her giftedness as a leader of senior executives, despite her relative youth.

She found the intersection of her giftedness (leadership) and her passion (problem solving). Plus, she loved new challenges. This skill set was the perfect combination for her to be promoted to the role of president of our newly formed European subsidiary, which began with no people, except Jane, and no properties. From these beginnings, she led our company's expansion into the operation, ownership, and development of over $2 billion worth of apartments in Germany, over the course of several years. We were the first publicly traded apartment company to expand outside of the U.S., and Jane's unique combination of giftedness and passions allowed us to do so very successfully. It was a very fulfilling and fun role for her for over eight years, and prepared her for other leadership roles following the sale of our company.

If you don't feel you have a complete understanding of the intersection of your passions and your giftedness, seek feedback from others around you as this is a critical element of personal discovery. While all feedback is useful, some is more important and valid than others. The important thing is to ask for feedback about yourself—your strengths, weaknesses, perceptions by others, work style, and other key areas—from as many different people as possible. Gather feedback from your peers, subordinates, and managers—as well as friends and family—in an effort to obtain a complete picture of yourself. The more information you collect, the better you will be able to find your personal intersection and maximize the satisfaction and performance from your career.

Another way to refine your understanding of your intersection is to identify a mentor who is committed to help you along in your journey. Some workplaces will actually help identify mentors for their employees, which can be an outstanding opportunity. If this situation is not available to you, consider asking someone you respect a great deal to be a mentor to you. Your mentor should be someone who has been successful with his own career and life choices, and is excited about investing in you. A good mentor will take the time to get to know you on a personal level, as well as to understand your workplace dynamics and challenges, and provide solid advice and counsel as you wrestle with important decisions. A mentor can help you make decisions about what career to pursue, when to leave your current position and seek something different, how to handle challenging situations at work, as well as at home, and many other key life decisions.

Some mentors stay with their mentee for a relatively short period of time, perhaps a year or two, while others stay involved for decades. A close relationship like this can be an

Pursuing a career at the intersection of your passions and giftedness will maximize your chances of success, fulfillment, and fun.

invaluable point of reference throughout your life, and is definitely worth taking the time to pursue.

Finding your intersection means having a willingness to explore new situations and opportunities. Don't be afraid to seek out new positions in an effort to better refine your knowledge of your intersection. Always continue to develop your skill set as you progress. Even though a new situation may not prove to be a good fit for you, the learning from this effort is invaluable, as it shows you an area or position to avoid as you make future career decisions. Finding your intersection is as much about crossing potential roles off your list, as it is about identifying those that might fit. Often decisions become much easier to make when we begin by eliminating things that are a definite NO, before working to select among those that are a possible YES.

Above all, realize how incredibly powerful finding your intersection can be to success and fulfillment in your career. Although it may take a lot of time up front to get it right, your effort will be richly rewarded throughout the rest of your life.

Pursuing a career at the intersection of your passions and giftedness will maximize your chances of success, fulfillment, and fun. In turn, an engaging career provides the platform from which to pursue passions in other areas of your life, which is the ultimate key to a life well-lived, regret-free life.

When finding the intersection of your passions and your giftedness, remember that:

1) Finding the ideal intersection of your passions and giftedness isn't easy, and can require considerable time and several different job experiences in order to arrive at the right answer.

2) Pursuing a career path at the intersection of your passions and your giftedness will maximize your opportunities for success, fulfillment, and fun in both your life and your career.

3) If possible, identify a mentor to assist in the process of identifying your intersection, as well as provide advice on important life decisions.

4) Seek continual feedback as you explore career options. Feedback is the key to self-understanding and self-improvement.

Chapter 4
Living Life with Fewer Regrets

We have already established that a life well-lived uses each day as an opportunity for continuous learning, both about yourself, and about the world around you. One of the best ways to learn is by tapping the knowledge of those who have gone before us in a given situation. As we all know, experience is the best teacher.

When I think about "maximizing my life," I think about making the most of each and every day. It is tempting to think that this means identifying ways to spend time more efficiently. However, while efficiency is an important emphasis, it isn't the most important tool in making the most out of each day. In fact, the most important focus is to identify the *right* things to invest our time in during each day that is given to us.

With this in mind, what can those who have gone before us teach us about this topic? When people who are nearing the end of their lives are asked, "What are your biggest regrets?," the most common answers are, "I wish I had spent more time with my family," and "I wish I had taken more risks." This is also expressed as I wish I had taken the risks needed to achieve my dreams and aspirations, tried more things outside of my comfort zone, been more willing to fail/be embarrassed while learning something new, and similar themes.

Even with this wisdom available to us, most achievement-oriented people find it difficult to live in a way that eliminates these two potential regrets from their lives. Career often supplants critically important time with family members, under the cover of, "I just need to work this hard now, and then (at some unspecified future time) I will be able to spend more time with my family." In turn, the fear of embarrassment or failure makes the decision to take the risk of pursuing your dreams and aspirations quite difficult for most people.

This chapter will address both of these potential regrets (which are also incredible life opportunities), but let's cover the topic of taking more risks first. Both of these issues presented significant challenges for me in my life and career, but the topic of taking more risks was one that I tackled in a particularly interesting way.

I already mentioned that I wasn't a very athletically oriented kid, and didn't experience my first success in athletics until college when I earned a spot on our collegiate tennis team. I practiced for hours each day in an effort to achieve this goal, and decided to take the risk of pursuing this dream, against what seemed like very long odds at the time.

Interestingly, this achievement gave me far more satisfaction than my exemplary academic record during my college career. The satisfaction came from trying something way outside of my comfort zone, with only a small chance of success. Despite the odds, I did succeed, which is something I have often reflected on as I have faced other difficult challenges in my life.

When I graduated from college, I still wasn't proficient at any sports besides golf and tennis. These two sports are only a small portion of the so-called, "lifetime sports" that are available as recreational opportunities for all of us. Not only are some of these lifetime sports great for camaraderie and relaxation, but they also can be wonderful ways to spend quality and quantity family time throughout the years.

Most people have familiarity, or proficiency, with a few of these sports (primarily from their youth), but once college is over, they cease to learn new sports. My theory is that when a person is invited by a friend to participate in a sport they are not familiar with, their typical response is, "Oh, thank you, but I am not really into (fill in the blank with skiing, tennis, surfing, etc.)." What they really mean is that they don't know how to do that particular sport, or don't know how to do it well enough (in their mind), so would rather avoid potential embarrassment, even though it might be a really fun outing with their friends. I fit this definition perfectly when I moved to Denver, Colorado for my first job after graduating from business school.

I was frequently invited to go snow skiing, and would typically demur, or otherwise avoid the invitation. I had skied a couple of times before, but was pretty hopeless at the sport, I figured it was best just to avoid it.

The problem was that skiing is by far the most popular sport for young, career-oriented people during the Colorado winters, and I was missing out on a lot of great friendship and camaraderie by not being a skier. After my first winter of saying no, I decided to take the risk of embarrassment and work hard to become a decent skier. I bought a pass, and some inexpensive skis, boots, and poles and went up to the mountains every weekend. I never became what I would call a great skier, but after much work, I became good enough to ski with my friends (even if I was the last one down the double black diamond runs) and have a great time.

This risk enabled me to look forward to the winter weekends, the great friendships, camaraderie, and sheer fun I got from skiing. I was 25 years old at the time and I had given this learning process a great deal of thought.

The most important takeaway for me was that trying something new (even though potentially embarrassing) was both interesting and stimulating. In addition, I learned that if I worked hard at developing a new skill, I could ultimately achieve enough proficiency to have fun with it. I also learned that it was incredibly fulfilling to learn new skills.

Because I had dreamed of being a good athlete nearly all of my life, but only saw myself as mediocre at best, I wasn't sure I'd be able to develop a competency at new sports, especially since I had played so few growing up. I made the bold decision that I would commit to learn one new sport each year until I turned 50. I decided to take the risk of becoming a good athlete, even though the odds seemed to be stacked against me.

Everyone probably has a similar experience in learning a sport for the first time. As you watch others who are proficient at the sport, they look relaxed, fluid, and graceful. It doesn't LOOK that difficult.

When it is YOUR turn to try it, everything is different. You are nervous, stiff, and uncomfortable, and the initial result is anything but graceful. Usually, there is a bit of frustration and embarrassment involved, and a realization that learning this new sport will be a lot harder than it looks.

Growing up in Southern California, I dreamed of learning to surf. Surfing was for those cool-looking, muscular guys who had perpetual tans. Of course, not being athletically inclined, I never tried it, as I was too nervous to take the plunge. After learning a new sport each year for over 10 years, I worked up the courage to try surfing, even though I was still living in Denver, far from the ocean.

My first surf outing is a vivid memory for me. As I walked down to the beach with my friend, Keith, the waves looked kind of small, and I wondered whether they would be big enough for learning. When I shared this sentiment with Keith, he laughed heartily, and said, "I'm not even sure you will be able to paddle out through these waves to get to where you will need to be to catch a wave."

But after 10 years of learning a new sport each year, I secretly thought to myself, "He is really underestimating me. I can swim and balance reasonably well, this will be no problem at all."

Of course, the reality was far different from my perception. I got on my board and began paddling confidently toward the breaking waves. Suddenly, those minor waves looked MUCH larger than they looked from the shore. As the first wave came racing toward me (much faster than I expected), I braced myself to be able to paddle through it and continue my journey to the outside.

A few seconds later found me knocked off my board, working hard to keep my head above water, and getting ready for the impact of the NEXT wave. And they just kept coming, one after another, after another. After swallowing a lot of water (along with my pride), I had been pushed back into the shallow water, looking out at the waves, realizing that paddling out was actually very, very difficult.

Keith asked again if I wanted some tips on getting out, which I readily accepted. With his instruction, I was able to make it out through the surf, after 15 minutes of steady, relentless paddling, a few falls off my board, and climbing back on as quickly as possible so as to not lose my hard-earned progress.

That was the good news. The bad news was that my arms and back muscles were exhausted, and I was breathing hard (I thought I was in good shape—perhaps for tennis, but not for surfing). Now, I had to try to catch a wave (also not as easy as it looks).

After all of this, when you finally catch a wave, you have to endure the indignity of trying to stand up on your board, again, and again, and again—only to experience a fleeting moment of glory before being plunged back into the surf and trying to avoid the impact of the board on your head, or other body parts.

As exhausting and humbling as my first two-hour surfing experience was, I absolutely fell in love with the sport and was determined to reach a level of proficiency that would allow me to pursue it with friends who were capable surfers. Many of them traveled to beautiful tropical destinations to surf, which, ultimately, became an annual trip for me, one I looked forward to with great anticipation.

It takes a lot of days in the water to learn to surf, and with my home being in Denver, it was an even greater challenge—or risk. There were many times when my good friends would tell me that I should just pick another sport to focus on, because surfing is so hard to learn as an adult—especially if you don't live on, or near, a beach.

Nevertheless, I persisted in my efforts and was ultimately rewarded with the ability to become a decent intermediate surfer. I have had the privilege to surf with friends, co-workers, and three of my children at many wonderful locations around the world.

Taking the risk of learning to surf in my late 30s, and working hard to overcome the odds against doing so, is one of a number of incredibly fulfilling stories I could share from my 25 years of learning new sports.

These experiences have broadened my horizons, and have provided great variety and accomplishment in my life. In addition, many of these sports have been amazing sources of quality time and incredible memories with my family, friends, and co-workers.

Of course, if I hadn't taken the initial risks of embarrassment and failure, I would have missed out on all of those fantastic benefits. I also always would have wondered, "What if I did try that, what would it have been like?"

Don't wonder what it would be like to try something, or to take an uncomfortable risk. Get wet! Your life will be much richer for the adventure!

While to this point, this chapter has discussed risk taking more in the personal side of our lives, the same sentiments hold true in our business careers. However, when you are running a company, or a division, deciding to take a risk will affect many more people than just yourself. As a consequence, these decisions must be weighed very carefully, before plunging headlong into unknown territory.

Nevertheless, the decisions to take calculated risks in a business context are absolutely essential if you are to build a business that is on the cutting edge of its industry and produces industry-leading performance.

In 1995, as our management team took over Archstone's predecessor company, Property Trust of America, we spent considerable time together to outline our plans and dreams for this relatively small, regional apartment company. We were taking over from a very well-regarded management team, which had operated from a pretty traditional playbook, and had produced excellent results. We all were relatively young (I was only 38, quite young to be leading a publicly traded company with over $1 billion in assets), and incredibly excited.

We spent time outlining our goals and objectives and decided that we were ready to take the risk of adopting some very lofty goals. The tagline we defined for ourselves was, "Leading the Real Estate Industry into New Territory." Certainly quite audacious!

Our industry was quite old-fashioned at the time. Very little technology was used in our business, and the prevailing wisdom was that you just bought apartment properties, or built them, as inexpensively as you could, and held on to them, essentially forever.

We decided to work to change some of those things—and when I say *some*, I mean *all!* We wanted to establish a branded identity in a business where, basically, there were no brands. We also wanted to implement technology to do outcomes-based credit scoring for new residents (at the time it was all done manually, and took 48 hours). Another big goal was to bring sophisticated revenue management to the pricing of our apartments, which would also allow us to lease apartments online (at the time, this was all done manually, at the property level, with reams of paperwork).

All the leaders in the industry told us that none (not "some," mind you) of our ideas would work. I'm pleased to say that we relentlessly pursued our objectives, and did completely redefine our industry. Today, all of these aforementioned initiatives were pioneered by Archstone and have become standard practice in the industry.

The successful pursuit of our aspirations and dreams for our small company (despite significant risks) provided tremendous satisfaction for our people and made them very proud to be Archstone associates. We enjoyed incredibly strong morale and employee engagement, and our culture was widely loved by our people.

These are only some of the many changes we made to the apartment industry. We also brought a key change to the overall real estate industry, which is the concept of capital recycling and continually improving your portfolio. Again, when we announced our desire to systematically sell our lower growth assets and move our capital to assets with better future growth prospects, investors opposed our strategy. Because of this, I endured a number of personal criticisms by industry analysts.

The beauty of this initiative was that we were doing the right thing for our shareholders, and eventually the superior growth produced by a continually improving portfolio became very obvious to analysts and, most importantly, to our shareholders. Today, capital recycling and continuous portfolio improvement are standard practice among publicly traded real estate companies, an enormous change that began with our team being willing to take a calculated risk.

Nearly all of the greatest memories and points of satisfaction from my 20 years of leadership at Archstone have come from either the thoughtful decisions to pursue risks (like those outlined above), or from the deep relationships developed over the years, which still continue today—three years after the sale of the company. The importance of relationships is discussed in greater detail in Chapter 8.

This chapter wouldn't be complete without a brief discussion of the importance of spending time with family. The failure to do so is often an individual's biggest regret in life, especially for senior business leaders. So, why is it so difficult to carve the time out of our schedules to do this?

For nearly all of those who don't spend enough time with their families, likely their spouse and children would still be placed at the top of their priority list, in theory. The challenge becomes trying to balance the continual demands that emanate from an ascendant career, and the feeling that if one doesn't devote extraordinary time and energy pursuing this, they will fall behind.

Certainly, there are tradeoffs. I had been with Security Capital Group (the largest shareholder and manager of Property Trust of America) for just two weeks when the chairman mentioned that the company was having a meeting on Sunday afternoon to work on a large transaction. I told him that Sunday is a day I have reserved for my family and apologized that I would be unable to attend. I also assured him that I was on top of the issues I had responsibility for and would have everything he needed available for review on Monday.

To be honest, I didn't think this would cost me my job. In fairness, I had told the company's senior executives during the interview process that I reserved weekends for my family, and although I was willing to do some work in the evenings, the day times were essential for me to be with our two young children. However, I did believe it would very likely impede my career advancement there. Notwithstanding the career risk, I believed that this decision reflected the personal priorities that were important to me, and was willing to accept the consequences to my career progression.

I made many of these decisions to prioritize time with my family at the risk of my career progression during my initial years at Security Capital Group, and it definitely had a short-term impact on my career there. I know this because the chairman told me it took him two years to get comfortable with giving me the position of overall responsibility for the company that became Archstone. He said that I was "unusual," and he wasn't sure that I was committed enough to my work to be successful in the role.

Of course, as we spent more time together, working on a multitude of transactions, he came to understand that he could count on me to get everything done that was needed, even if I sometimes left the office early to coach one of my children's sports teams, or to attend a school performance. I worked hard, but I organized my schedule so that I could spend substantial time with my family. It was a very deliberate decision to establish priorities that would ensure I would never regret not spending enough time with my family.

But let me take this a step farther. Spending time with your family doesn't just mean showing up for occasional dinners, or seeing your children on weekends in between golf games. It means spending the time needed to understand what is important to each of them, and doing your best to participate in those activities.

Coaching sports teams for your children is a wonderful way to spend time with them, if they (and you) are interested in this. If this doesn't fit your family situation, then certainly attending your children's sports games, school functions, and similar activities is essential.

The requirements for success here are the same as they are for any relationship—understand what is important to the person you are trying to spend time with, and then immerse yourself in it with them—caring enough to listen and learn.

The same rules apply to spending quality time with your spouse. Understand the priorities, goals, activities, and topics of conversation that are important to your spouse. Of course, the obvious challenge is that these may not be the items that are important to you! However, if you spend time doing activities that are important to your spouse, your spouse will ultimately reciprocate.

Certainly, I will acknowledge that there are a number of jobs that simply don't allow those tradeoffs to be made, while still retaining your position. The questions you need to ask, if you decide to pursue a job like this, are: (a) Do I only want to do this job until I have children, and then transition into

The requirements for success here are the same as they are for any relationship—understand what is important to the person you are trying to spend time with, and then immerse yourself in it with them.

something else? (b) Is continuing to stay in this job after I have children worth the regret of not seeing my family enough?

These are challenging questions with no right answer. I'm certain I could have made a lot more money than I have made, or run a much larger company than I did, but as I mentioned earlier, I made deliberate tradeoffs. I have aimed to lead a very purposeful and carefully considered life, and throughout my career I have made many tough decisions using pre-established priorities and values. I can say with tremendous confidence that, if I had it to do over again, I wouldn't do it any other way.

The important point to remember is that there are tradeoffs to be made. Spending the time up front to carefully articulate your priorities, in light of the reality of potential future regrets, will allow you to make informed decisions about these pivotal tradeoffs.

Making tradeoffs in the allocation of our time and energy is one of the most challenging things we do, and the decisions we make today will often have important consequences many years in the future. As you make these important decisions, endeavor to:

1) Allocate both quality and quantity time to those who are closest to you.

2) Identify ways to challenge yourself regularly by trying completely new experiences. Remember, it is okay to look or feel awkward, and it is very fun to learn new skills.

3) Experience the joy of learning. It strengthens every part of you, and emboldens you to take on the next new challenge.

4) Find someone to pursue new experiences with. It is fun to share the joy of accomplishments and the embarrassment of new challenges with other people.

Chapter 5
The "As Soon As" Mentality

The "as soon as" mentality is a relatively easy concept to understand, but a very difficult reality to change. True change in this area requires thoughtful prioritization, careful planning, and deliberate actions. Without all three, you will still find yourself saying, "as soon as...," in the twilight of your life.

What do I mean by this concept? Simply stated, most people have a long list of things they would love to do. Perhaps it is spending more time at their vacation home, taking a trip to an exotic destination, learning a foreign language, or something as simple as taking a trip to visit an important relative. When asked when they will do this, the typical response is, "as soon as I have _____," fill in the blank with any number of things, such as, closed the next deal, achieved my promotion, saved more money, or innumerable others.

The challenge is that for many people, "as soon as" never comes. There always seems to be another reason to wait or delay. Sadly, you wake up one day and find that you aren't able to pursue your dreams any more (perhaps due to health reasons, or any number of other impediments).

How do we avoid this trap?

First, we must prioritize our dreams and goals. This prioritization should include career, personal, family, and recreational goals. What is truly most important to you? How does this issue relate in importance to the next item on your list? Which goals have specific time frames associated with them, and which goals are more general in nature? What goals are you willing to defer, or even sacrifice, so that you can achieve those that are of the highest priority to you?

When we engage in a thoughtful prioritization process outside of the stresses of daily life, and then take the time to revisit it regularly, we provide ourselves with clarity of vision. This clarity of vision allows us to make the difficult scheduling tradeoffs needed to ensure that we are focusing our time on those areas we have deemed to be our highest priorities, and not just getting sucked into endless hours of task-oriented requirements fed by inertia.

One exercise I did at least annually was to chart the way I spent my time (during 15-minute intervals) throughout a given week for all 24 hours of each day of the week. The results allowed me to understand how much time I was spending on different segments of my life, and how this time allocation aligned with my stated priorities. When this process revealed that I was spending too little time on a key priority, then I had to make some difficult decisions. It is impossible to add more than 24 hours to a day (I can't count the times I'd wished I could extend the day another hour or two), so in order to spend more time on one area of my life, I had to decrease the time I spent on another area of my life. The correct answer is to make these decisions based on your previously articulated priorities, but it is usually more challenging to do this than one would expect—particularly given the inertia of an existing schedule, as well as the expectations of others.

For me, the area of my life that often got reduced was my time for sleep. I was very fortunate that, as a younger man (in my 30s and 40s), I was able to function on very little sleep, often as little as three hours per night. I'm not necessarily advocating this approach, but my body was wired so that I was able to make it work well, and in so doing, add some extra hours to my day for pursuing other priorities.

I also pursued a similar time allocation discipline for my calendar year. I was fortunate to have four weeks of annual paid vacation, and I was very deliberate at ensuring that I availed my family of this opportunity to be together, and enjoy time with each other. We would spend time selecting places we wanted to visit, researching them, and then turn this research into a reality.

We didn't have a vacation home until my oldest child, Danielle, was 5. We purchased a small two bedroom condominium across the street from the beach in Del Mar, California. The kids loved the beach, and I loved to share it with them. I also loved the opportunity to work on my surfing early in the morning before my family got up to start the day. I could spend 90 minutes enjoying the total relaxation of surfing, and be showered and changed in time to have breakfast with everyone.

Our company had made the decision to establish a significant presence in California by that time, so I arranged my schedule to be able to live at our Del Mar condo for at least one month every summer, working during the day from our condo, or the local office, but doing so on an abbreviated schedule in order to spend ample time with my family. We built incredible memories over the years in the condo, and our family still loves going there for vacations.

I believe that time away from the office is absolutely essential to the germination of new ideas, keeping you fresh and engaged, and making you more productive and efficient with the time you spend in the office. Some of our company's best strategic ideas emanated from time I spent on "vacation." However, I would also note that as a senior executive, your mind

When we engage in a thoughtful prioritization process outside of the stresses of daily life, and then take the time to revisit it annually, we provide ourselves with clarity of vision.

is always tuned into the channel of your brain that reflects on your business. During parts of the day, this channel is on pause in the background, as you spend time with family, play sports, or other leisure activities, but still, deep in the recesses of your mind, you are subconsciously processing ideas that relate to your position at work. Getting away from the confines of the office allows you to think much more expansively about things, and often leads to important breakthroughs.

My point in all of this is that it took very purposeful prioritization and planning in order to identify a place that my family would enjoy, and then ensure that we allocated the time to visit it regularly. Deliberate advance planning and frequent monitoring of my schedule and priorities created this time away.

All of us know people who have lovely vacation homes and rarely use them. They dream of using them someday, or, "as soon as." We hear many stories of people who retire, excited to enjoy their newfound free time, only to be hobbled by health issues and unable to pursue their dreams.

It is essential not to wait to pursue our important dreams and goals. Our lives are short and our health isn't guaranteed. If we are constantly putting things off until we "have time," we will very likely never do them. As human beings, our inclination is to settle into established habits and schedules and rarely step away to scrutinize the time we allocate to various pursuits.

I encourage you to make the decision to be different, and live a carefully examined and thoughtfully prioritized life. You will be richly blessed by doing so.

A RELATED "AS SOON AS" TRAP

Another area of our lives where we often miss opportunities is in following up our casual conversations with purposeful actions. How often have you met someone interesting at a function and mentioned something like, "We should get together sometime," only to never follow up and do so. These are important missed opportunities.

Instead, establish the discipline that if you mention getting together with someone, you will commit to follow up within 24 hours to establish a date and time to connect. You will often find that people are shocked by your prompt follow up, but also are flattered and excited to make the connection. Of course, the corollary to this is to scrupulously avoid insincere small talk about getting together with someone whom you don't really want to spend time with. I have found both of these disciplines to be very rewarding.

One interesting example from early in my career is instructive. In 1984, at a closing dinner for two apartment transactions we had recently completed, our banker, our lawyer, and I (we were all single men at the time) were discussing places in the world we wanted to see. During the conversation, the idea of a trip to Africa came up, and our lawyer mentioned that he had spent two great years in Kenya with a pharmaceutical company and would really like to go back and climb Mt. Kilimanjaro. We all talked about how fun it would be to do this (but, of course, our banker and lawyer were thinking in the time frame of "as soon as ____").

I picked up the phone to call each of them the next morning, and asked when they could free up their schedules to go to Africa. I spoke with them separately, but each of them was shocked that I was actually serious about the trip. When I asked them if they wanted to go, they replied with an enthusiastic, "Yes!" but just didn't know when they could get away.

It took several weeks of calling, vetting possible dates and ideas, and cajoling each of them before they agreed to schedule a trip 13 months away. We had an amazing time together, and that trip was one of the highlights of my young life. Being on top of the highest point in Africa was a surreal feeling, and I enjoyed it so much that I did it again nearly 30 years later.

I fell in love with the terrain, wildlife, and people of Africa, and have returned many times since. I'm not sure I would have ever gone to visit Africa if I hadn't made the time to go then, when I had the initial opportunity. Had I not done so, I would have missed some of my most memorable travel experiences.

Life is short, relationships are deeply meaningful, and inertia exerts a very strong pull. Don't wait for "as soon as!" Do important things now!

Chapter 6
Stand Up and Do What is Right—
Even in the Face of Criticism

There have been countless experiments done to document the extraordinary power of peer pressure. Perhaps you remember the classroom experiment where the teacher shows the class three lines, with one being obviously longer than the other two, and asks the class to vote on which line is the longest. Unknown to one student, everyone else in the class has already been briefed to vote for the second longest line, leaving this one student as the lone vote for the longest line.

What happens the majority of the time? Ultimately, this one student looks around at the others in the class, who are voting for one of the shorter lines, and changes his vote to be consistent with the rest of the class, even though it is clear he is voting for the shorter line.

Why is peer pressure so powerful? We have an innate desire to fit in, to get along with others, and not to look like an outlier in the crowd. To take the road less traveled is a brave choice. It takes tremendous conviction to make the initial choice, and even more conviction to stay the course, as the criticism increases the longer we remain on a different path.

The important thing to remember is that if you decide to pursue a different path from the commonly accepted approach, regardless of what walk of life it is in, you will experience criticism and significant pressure to change, or to conform.

Of course, this makes it all the more important that your position on any given issue is well researched, carefully evaluated, and thoughtfully considered. Beliefs, especially controversial ones, should be espoused when you have a high degree of confidence in your position, and are capable of eloquently explaining your particular opinion.

An excellent case in point, from my experience, are the challenges we faced when using a long-term perspective to run a public company instead of the typical emphasis on quarterly earnings.

Running a publicly traded company is difficult. You have a plethora of critics, including stock analysts, whose job it is to identify flaws in your plans, strategy, execution, or performance and write compelling articles about these mistakes that will garner attention.

Investors are continually looking for the best places to allocate their capital, which means that you need to identify how your company stands out from the host of other companies they can invest in. Competitors are constantly looking for ways to outmaneuver you, and your employees are being heavily recruited by other companies in the continual battle among all employers to attract and retain the very best talent. These are all among the long list of challenges for a public company CEO.

However, despite all of these challenges, I believe the most difficult challenge of all is making strategic decisions that will create long-term value, but may depress short-term earnings and performance.

The public equity markets in the U.S. are strongly oriented around the quarterly performance cycle. Every three months, public companies must report their earnings and other key metrics. An enormous industry has been built around estimating these quarterly performance statistics and looking for any hints, no matter how subtle, of what these metrics might look like next quarter, or the quarter after that. Reporting earnings that are even slightly below what are referred to as "analyst consensus estimates" (essentially, the average estimated earnings number of all the analysts that follow a given company), can cause an immediate and substantial decline in a company's share price. Add to that, it can take months—or years—to recover from a decline of this kind.

We had more than 20 Wall Street analysts following our company. They were typically young and whip-smart, and looking to make a name for themselves as savvy prognosticators of a given company's future. That being said, I found nearly every one of them to strongly favor very traditional approaches to company strategy, and be very vocal in their opposition to anything outside of standard operating procedure.

Moreover, there is such a strong emphasis on the achievement of steadily growing quarterly earnings—both among analysts and many investors—that pursuing strategies that would create long-term value at the expense of current earnings was nearly certain to evoke exceptionally strong criticism.

As noted in my 1998 letter to shareholders, we didn't plan to pursue standard operating procedure in running Archstone. We wanted to reinvent the real estate industry, and we actually meant it. I noted:

> *What I would like to do in my letter, and in our annual report, is to help you better understand Archstone's business plan, personality, and culture—and how they set us apart in our rapidly changing industry.*
>
> *Simply stated, we are leading the real estate industry into new territory. Conventional wisdom has been that*

success in real estate is measured by transaction volume and deal-making. This simply is not the case. Long-term success in our industry is driven by the same fundamentals that provide the foundation for any other successful company: to operate an outstanding business that understands and serves its customers. At Archstone, we are committed to earning the right to be viewed as a leader in the service business, not solely as an owner and operator of apartment communities.

I believe that our commitment to provide our customers with consistent service that exceeds their expectations will allow Archstone to build a powerful national brand, the first in the apartment industry...We are confident that creating value for our customers also creates significant value for our shareholders.

In addition to the value created through our relentless commitment to operational excellence, prudent balance sheet management, and a disciplined investment strategy provide distinct advantages for Archstone. Ours is a capital-intensive business, and we consider capital a scarce resource that must be invested selectively, with a consistent strategy.

First, we want our capital invested in locations where it is very difficult to build competing product—in other words, where there are "barriers to entry." Limited competition produces better long-term growth that is internally generated, requiring little incremental capital.

We do not purchase assets to achieve size objectives. In fact, when it makes sense to sell assets that no longer meet our investment criteria, we do so. We do this to avoid raising incremental common equity—which dilutes our shareholders' ownership in Archstone—and to ensure our

capital is always invested in the best possible growth op-
portunities...In our view, investing only for accretion is a
flawed business strategy that does not produce enduring
value.

(I should add here that this strategic direction outlined in my 1998 letter remained unchanged for the next 15 years, through the sale of the company in 2013.)

The fundamental differences in our strategy, when compared with the traditional approaches to real estate, were:

1. We believed that we could use professional operations, a significant investment in technology and the creation of an exceptionally positive culture to build a differentiated operating platform, which would produce substantial long-term value for shareholders. (Conventional wisdom was that real estate operations were a functional necessity, but not a source of differentiation, and therefore, not worth investing in.)

2. We believed that owning real estate in markets where it was very difficult to build new housing was the key to creating the best long-term growth and value for shareholders. Archstone didn't own that type of real estate when we assumed managerial responsibility for the company, so we had to sell all of what we owned, and invest the proceeds into the type of real estate we wanted to own for the long term. The enormous challenge with this was that the assets we currently owned were valued at lower multiples of cash flow than the assets we wanted to own for the long term.

Therefore, every time we sold an existing asset and redeployed the capital into our targeted asset type, we reduced our current earnings, which made us extremely unpopular.

3. We were focused on creating long-term value from the real estate we owned, as opposed to maximizing current earnings. This meant that we were willing to consider merger and acquisition transactions that might be initially dilutive to current earnings, if they produced better long-term growth and value creation. The willingness to consummate a dilutive merger transaction was perhaps the most controversial position of all.

The CEO of a large public company who is followed by more than 20 Wall Street analysts is able to read something printed about the company, and/or its management, nearly every single business day. It is true that if you read your own press you are likely to either become too sensitive to the criticism, or become too confident in your own abilities (in the event you are receiving positive feedback). However, you do need to read a good number of the analyst reports published on your company in order to be prepared to answer the myriad of questions from investors that will be generated by them.

It is not easy to read headlines like, "What Kind of Kool-Aid Is Management Drinking?" and "Sellers Is a Serial Diluter," and many others of similar ilk. When your strategy, intellect, vision, and business understanding are repeatedly questioned in a very visible public forum—day after day, for several years—it is hard to stay the course, but that is exactly what we did.

We did this because we fervently believed that the approach we had articulated was right, and would create the most long-term value for our shareholders, even if it would take years to prove the validity of our approach.

It is important to note that we never would have been able to pursue these goals without the unwavering support of our board of directors. The board read the same critical analyst reports, and certainly asked us questions about our strategy, but it believed strongly in the vision we had articulated to them at the beginning of the implementation of our long-term strategic plan, and had the courage to stand behind us. Without the board's strong support, we never could have executed the dramatic turnaround of the company that we ultimately achieved.

It took over seven years for the chorus of repeated criticism to begin to turn, even if those levels of admiration and praise were only faint at first. Nine years after we started our turnaround, we received virtually nothing but glowing reports from the analyst community, and were one of the "darlings" among publicly traded real estate companies. It felt very good for all of our associates to realize that everything we had all worked so hard for over the course of nine years was finally paying off, and had literally changed how people in the real estate industry think about their businesses.

If you look at the public real estate industry today, the three points of our strategy that once were so contrary to standard operating procedure, are now fully embraced as the best practices for real estate businesses. This is true not only for apartment companies, but also for those in the retail, office, industrial, and hotel businesses. Our willingness to stand up and do what was right (even in the face of sustained criticism) was a catalyst to changing the real estate industry.

Having the courage to pursue your convictions is an essential component of living a satisfied life, a life with as few regrets as possible.

Of course, the result of doing what is right, even in the face of criticism, doesn't always produce a storybook ending like this. However, having the courage to pursue your convictions is an essential component of living a satisfied life, a life with as few regrets as possible.

The same maxim of standing up and doing what is right, even in the face of criticism, also applies to our personal lives. Peer pressure is so powerful, that it is very easy to be molded into the beliefs and habits of those around you, without even realizing it is happening.

At every stage of our lives we need to establish priorities and guidelines for how we intend to spend our time, and continually monitor our progress to ensure we are following the priorities we established. For example, if it is a priority for you to donate some time to give back to the community each month, you can be sure there will be many options that will consume your schedule, leaving no spare time for community service. The only way to ensure that you consistently devote adequate time to your priority of community service, is to specifically schedule it into your agenda, preferably weeks in advance.

The same thing is true with exercise. Nearly everyone wants to be fit and in shape, but, as life progresses, fewer and fewer people actually attain this objective. In my opinion, there are two primary reasons for this:

(a) Exercise usually fits in the schedule when we have spare time, which for most of us is virtually never, and

(b) Exercise is hard work. Too often we decide that maintaining our fitness simply isn't worth it, or is too difficult to add to our busy schedule.

The point is not that everyone should be fit. However, if it is an important priority for you, exercise must be deliberately placed in your daily schedule, or you simply won't do it. If you do make exercise a priority, you can be sure you will be criticized for taking so much time for fitness (because most people don't), but you will be personally rewarded for staying the course.

Similarly, if you decide to make anything an important priority in your life (e.g., learning an instrument, attending weekly worship services, sharing your time in community service, or countless other examples), you are certain to experience criticism for allocating substantial time to anything that differs materially from the schedules and priorities of those around you. Don't be discouraged by this, and certainly don't give up on your own priorities. Over time you will be rewarded with satisfaction and accomplishment by adhering to the priorities you establish.

Being true to your priorities and values establishes a strong reputation with others around you for dependability, consistency, and integrity. In this world of scandals and schemes, people are looking for those they can trust. Trust is developed through consistency of behavior, and decisions based on honesty and integrity. When others around you know that you will respond to a given situation in a dependable and honest manner, you build strong bonds of trust and a desirable reputation.

Building a reputation of honesty, integrity, and dependability is one of the most satisfying outcomes our lives can produce.

Chapter 7
Leadership Is All About Serving Others

The prototypical characterization of a leader is often a bold, charismatic individual who is tough, disciplined, and resolute. While these qualities can be helpful to leadership, in my experience, the single most important quality of a strong leader is the commitment to serve those around him.

When the associates who work for you believe that you care about them as individuals, and have a strong desire to help them succeed, they become fiercely loyal to you. If the entire company embodies this commitment of caring and supporting its associates, a strong culture of tremendous loyalty and performance is built from this foundation.

A strong foundation begins with articulating a set of core values that will define your culture. The most important thing about values is that you truly live them, from the top of the company all the way down the hierarchy, so they become real and meaningful to your team.

Very shortly after our team assumed managerial responsibility for Archstone, we articulated a simple, but profound set of values that would define our culture from the time we assumed responsibility for the company, until it was ultimately sold, nearly 20 years later. We began by agreeing that these were values we wanted to have as foundational elements of our workplace, regardless of what business we were in. Our values, and what they meant to us, are summarized below:

- Honest and Ethical – Without this as a hallmark of our culture, nothing else matters. We want to be true to our word in all circumstances.

- Leadership – We want to be the very best at what we do. We have a passion for excellence, and are focused on continuous improvement.

- Camaraderie – We enjoy spending time with each other, and want to have fun as we work together and serve our stakeholders. Work should be fun and enjoyable, as well as substantive.

- Innovative – We enjoy change, and will continually explore new and better ways to do things. Technology is a leading element of business improvement, and we want to find new and better ways for our customers to do business with us.

- Entrepreneurial Spirit – We will cultivate and retain an entrepreneurial approach to our business, despite how large we grow. We will be creative, thoughtful, and willing to take risks.

We recruited people who felt our values resonated with their approach to life and work. I would often tell our associates, "Recruit people for our team who have a passion to serve others." We would much rather train a new person who already has a passion to serve others, than to try to develop a passion for service in someone who knows the business, but lacks that passion.

We talked about the importance of our values with all of our associates at every meeting we had, as well as on our all-associate calls, which we held several times each year. I believe that we truly did live out our values in the workplace, the result of which was a very strong, supportive culture with an incredible passion for excellence and achievement. Our culture energized and inspired each and every one of us, and allowed us to achieve far more together than we would ever have been able to accomplish separately.

The best way to understand our culture is to hear from the associates who lived it each and every day. I should also add that since our company was sold in 2013 (the subject of a later chapter), none of the individuals quoted here currently work for me, or the company, so have no incentive to discuss anything but their sincere feelings about the company we used to work for.

> *Great culture starts with great leadership at the top of the organization.*
>
> *At Archstone, our leaders modeled the behavior they expected. We invested the time, money, and resources into bringing in people that fit the Archstone culture. In order to find the best people with a desire to provide strong customer service, we built custom assessment tools for each and every position. We determined the characteristics and skill set required for each and every position in the company. Our culture was one of transparency, honesty, and camaraderie. We worked hard and we played hard. We built a company that we could be proud of and enjoyed each and every day.*
>
> *—Jeanne Lynch, SVP and Head of Human Resources*

To me, the most important thing about Archstone was its culture. Having worked at several large, national apartment development companies prior to joining Archstone, I can say firsthand that Archstone's culture was truly unique. The emphasis that senior management placed on culture was, I believe, unmatched in the industry. Our exceptional culture touched every aspect of the company and made Archstone a wonderful place to work.

The first and foremost element of the Archstone culture was honesty and trust, followed closely by respect for your colleagues at all levels of the organization. Our culture of camaraderie and honesty produced outstanding results and created a remarkable work environment.

We focused on hiring talented people, gave them the latitude to make decisions, and nurtured their growth through mentorship. The results of this focus were that Archstone was a very special place to work. This, in turn, created tremendous loyalty and outstanding long-term results.

—Neil Brown, Chief Development Officer/EVP
Responsible for all of Archstone's developments nationwide

As you focus on serving those around you, not only will you substantially improve your leadership skills, but you will experience extraordinary satisfaction from the doing so.

The Archstone culture was directly linked to our core values. Our values were known and embraced up and down the organization. It was widely recognized that the culture came to life through shared values—the foundation upon which Scot and his leadership team built the company. Treating our internal and external customers with respect, kindness, empathy, and clear communication were always our highest priorities.

A healthy culture, modeled by the values of our leadership team, created a climate that fostered genuine relationships. When we're surrounded by like-minded people with shared values, we look forward to coming to work and are highly engaged. This, in turn, allows us to make a positive difference in the lives of our customers and our colleagues.

—Teresa Dalsager, Vice President Training and Leadership Development, Archstone Western Region

Clearly, these testimonials represent passionate feelings about the company and its culture. This is the passion that allowed us to overachieve, producing industry-leading property performance for many consecutive years.

A passionate culture, focused on excellence, allows a company to pursue a bold, ambitious vision. Our vision was to reinvent the real estate industry, and we all passionately pursued that objective together.

Many companies are averse to change. Change is difficult and requires a lot of hard work. You need to try some things that won't work, and then try again. This is disruptive and adds to the overall workload. However, the successful implementation of innovative change is unbelievably rewarding.

Our associates embraced change. In fact, they lived for it. They all wanted to know the next way we could pursue a reinvention of standard industry practices. The result was a fast-paced, highly energized workplace, which was always ready to take on something new. As a result of the incredible teamwork of our associates, Archstone was the first company in our industry to introduce a vast array of new initiatives to our business:

1. Capital recycling by selling slower growth assets and moving the capital to those assets with more optimal long-term growth.

2. Emphasis on the importance of investing in markets with very limited land on which new housing can be built ("protected markets").

3. Algorithmic credit approval process for prospective residents.

4. Sophisticated revenue management system for pricing rents.

5. Fully automated on-line leasing process.

6. Nationwide apartment company branding.

7. College degrees required for on-site apartment management roles.

8. Continual portfolio improvement, while raising minimal new common equity.

Not only was all of this incredibly gratifying to everyone, but we also had a great deal of fun working closely together to accomplish all of this.

A strong, supportive culture with a passion for excellence is the single most important ingredient of success that any business can have in its favor. When you look at an underperforming business, it nearly always has a weak, poorly motivated culture, which is the first thing that must be corrected in a turnaround effort.

Strong cultures start at the top, and a true leader is focused on serving those around him, which in turn creates the strong culture. This, in turn, generates a powerful competitive advantage.

Why is leadership that is focused on serving others so powerful and inspiring? Simply stated, everyone has goals and dreams for his life, and most of us fear that we may not be able to achieve a good many of our goals and dreams. When a leader or manager asks us about our personal objectives, and takes an interest in helping us achieve them, it is tremendously compelling. We feel we have someone we can work with, who is on our side, which is the foundation of strong teamwork.

A good leader also gives people an overarching sense of purpose and vision for their work. A sense of purpose increases dedication, fulfillment and overall job satisfaction. Perhaps you have heard the anecdote of the three men working in a limestone quarry, each with the same job.

The first one is asked what he is doing, and replies, "Breaking these large stones into smaller ones, as I am instructed." He worked hard, but saw his role as simply a job to earn money to pay the bills.

The second one is asked what he is doing, and replies, "I'm cutting limestone blocks of exquisite quality that will sell for

At the end of our lives, we will savor and treasure the deep relationships we have built, however, the awards and accolades accomplished along the way will be distant, faded memories.

premium prices." He worked even harder than the first man, and enjoyed his job, because he was making a product of high quality, but didn't feel a great sense of fulfillment, from his job.

The third one is asked what he is doing, and replies, "I'm building a cathedral that will glorify God and last for centuries as an architectural monument." This man loved his job and worked extra hours to ensure the cathedral would be truly magnificent when completed. He saw his job as part of a grander purpose and was excited to participate each day in something special, and much larger than himself.

Although this is a fictional story, I believe it captures the essence of what employees are looking for from their jobs and careers. Each of us has a strong desire for a *purpose*, to be part of something larger than ourselves. Creating a workplace in which employees feel bonded to the achievement of an important overarching goal, produces incredible employee satisfaction and makes work exceptionally rewarding.

All of us are in positions of leadership in different areas of our lives, and a focus on serving those around us will be a powerful source of differentiation for our leadership responsibilities. Not only does this create strong loyalty and teamwork among those we are leading, but it also is incredibly gratifying to those in leadership roles.

The benefits of serving those around us can also be extended to the personal side of our lives, as we dedicate some of our time to serve others in the world who have been less fortunate than we have been. I have never met a person who has spent time in service to others who hasn't felt they have received more than they have given during their time of service.

As you focus on serving those around you, not only will you substantially improve your leadership skills, but you will experience extraordinary satisfaction from the doing so.

Chapter 8
Life Is All About Relationships

Each of us ultimately decides what the focus of our life will be. Do we pursue achievements, titles, power, money, fun, leisure, family, or something else?

What we focus our lives on has profound consequences for us, because each day we spend is gone forever, unable to be relived. The importance of this reality becomes increasingly visible to us with each passing year. We will all get to the point where we have fewer years ahead of us than we have behind us, and the direction we have taken along the way becomes increasingly difficult to alter.

With the gravity of the focus of our lives in mind, what is the proper emphasis? I would submit that it is the development, nurturing, and maturity of relationships in our lives. At the end of our lives, we will savor and treasure the deep relationships we have built, however, the awards and accolades accomplished along the way will be distant, faded memories.

We already discussed the most important area of life for relationship development in Chapter 4—our family. Perhaps the most difficult relationships for rapidly rising young executives to nurture are those with our children. The cruel reality is that most of us start a family just at the point where our careers are becoming ascendant, and we delude ourselves into thinking that we can somehow make up later in life for the time we are not spending with our children now. Unfortunately, nothing could be further from the truth.

There is a prevalent myth that quality time, even in very small increments, is much more important than quantity time. Unfortunately, our children wouldn't agree with this notion. They want as much time with us as they can possibly get. It is this quantity time that builds the deep relationships with them that will endure the ups and downs of life and withstand the test of time.

Young children want to share their passions with their parents. Perhaps one of the most challenging things for me to embrace when my children were younger was that I needed to meet them where they were, instead of trying to convince them to enjoy the things I would rather do. A couple of examples may be helpful:

I loved playing tennis and golf, and although I tried to get my young son, Ross, interested in both of these sports, he decided he preferred soccer and basketball (two sports I had almost never played, and knew very little about). To be honest, I wasn't really interested in learning either of these sports, but because of Ross's interest in them, I spent time nearly every day after work kicking the soccer ball with him in the yard, or playing basketball in the driveway, or the gym.

He got into organized sports at the age of six, and his team needed a coach, so I volunteered. I ended up coaching a total of four sports that I knew next to nothing about at the outset (he also played football for two years and lacrosse for three years), from the time he was six until he was 13.

It wasn't too difficult to coach kids' sports when they were six, but by the time they are 10 or 11, it starts to become relatively sophisticated. I spent time reading up on plays, skills development, practice drills, and strategy, as well as practicing with Ross and his friends on off days, and running the weekly practices.

Ross is now 24 years old, and as we look back on our years together, these are some of our favorite memories. This time together created a special bond between us, which has grown even more meaningful as he has become a young man.

I am thankful to say that when we get together today, Ross now wants to play tennis and golf with me, as well as go snowboarding together (in keeping with the message in Chapter 4, and in pursuing those activities that allow you to connect with your kids, I began the embarrassing process of learning to snowboard at the ripe age of 50—definitely taking a risk, in more ways than one).

Ross and I have a great time, and also discuss very deep life issues together. I'm convinced that the building of our relationship started with meeting him where he was during his younger years—showing interest in that which interested him, and spending *quantity* time with him.

An even more interesting example is with my oldest daughter, Danielle, who is 27 today, and gifted artistically (she is an excellent singer, painter, and artist). By contrast, I have very little artistic background or skill. So meeting Danielle where her interests were was even more challenging for me. I learned about dancing, acting, singing, drawing, and painting, and even tried my hand at a few of them (embarrassing myself in the process, of course).

One of Danielle's favorite things to do when she was between 11 and 14 years old was to go to a restaurant near our home that had a karaoke night once a week, and sing together with me, up on the stage. (That combines the risk taking element from Chapter 4, as well as connecting with your children where they are!) We had so much fun together, and it really enhanced her confidence about performing in front of an audience. We created fantastic memories from those times together.

She is 27 today, and we still go on stage together to sing karaoke from time to time.

Perhaps these are silly examples, but the objective is to illustrate two very important points—don't miss the chance to connect with your children, especially when they are young, *and* to meet them where they are. You, and they, will be richly rewarded with incredibly meaningful lifelong relationships.

Of course, it goes without saying that investing the time to establish a deep, loving relationship with your spouse is one of the most important objectives of our emphasis on relationships. The ultimate goal is for our spouse to be our closest friend and confidant, a safe refuge from the challenges that life throws at us. This takes work, and selflessness, but if we can build this type of marriage relationship, it makes everything else in our life that much better.

What about relationships beyond our families? How important are they? Do we invest in these, too?

The answer is an unequivocal "yes!" Of all of the wonderful things to come out of my 20-year experience at Archstone, the relationships built there are by far the most important and meaningful to me outside of my family, and (based on all of the feedback I have seen) to our associates, as well.

As already mentioned, our objective was to understand the goals and dreams of those we worked with, and to help them achieve these objectives. In addition, our emphasis on camaraderie as a foundational value produced a cohesive culture in which we were able to get to know each other on a deeper, more meaningful level.

The results of this emphasis on relationships in my own life are very gratifying. Over the last five years, our family has taken five trips to Cambodian villages with Habitat for Humanity to build homes, toilets, and wells for less fortunate families there. On each of these trips, Archstone colleagues and their families have accompanied my family and me to work side by side, getting our hands dirty and our clothes drenched with sweat, as we labored together in the humid Cambodian summer. It was one thing when my colleagues joined me when the company still existed and we all worked together (2012), but even more amazing when former colleagues and their families joined us in subsequent years (2013, 2014, 2015, and 2016).

We used to love working together at the same company, but now we are friends who share a common experience and enjoy each other's company. When we get together we share our goals and challenges with each other, seeking advice and counsel, and have great fun together. That is the magic of building relationships. They endure beyond the current situation and provide a strong framework for our future.

Life is far more fun when shared, than when pursued individually. So endeavor to go deep in your relationships, and make it a key focus for your life. Remember, true relationships are enduring, but the awards and accolades are soon to be forgotten.

We can't choose our circumstances, but we can choose the attitude with which we face them.

Chapter 9
Life Is Not Always Fair

Wouldn't it be nice if everyone always got what they deserved (or perhaps I should say, what they think they deserve), hard work was always commensurately rewarded, and those who bend the rules didn't prosper? Unfortunately, we live in a world where this is not the reality of life. All of us can cite numerous examples of life simply not being fair.

Perhaps the more interesting question is why we think life should be fair? Of course, the corollary (and even more difficult) question is to define fair. Very often, what is fair for one person may be seen by another to be less than fair, which is perhaps why the best attitude with which to approach life is to *do our very best in everything we undertake*, but not expect life to treat us fairly. We should expect the unexpected, and be willing to adapt to whatever curve balls life throws at us, while always endeavoring to maintain a positive attitude.

When we are faced with a difficult circumstance, it is tempting to feel sorry for ourselves, and to bemoan the events that led us to this situation. If we emphasize the negative aspects of our life, we will likely become discouraged, and have a more difficult time harnessing the inner energy needed to deal with our challenges. If we choose to focus on the unfairness of the situation, we become victims of our circumstances, instead of finding ways to overcome them.

As difficult circumstances conspire to drag me down, I endeavor to make a conscious decision to focus on the points outlined below:

1. Make a list of the things I am thankful for, and center my thoughts on the gratitude for those blessings in my life.

2. Remember the people who are taking cues from my attitude and demeanor—which reinforces my responsibility to model a positive outlook for each of them.

3. Reflect on other difficult challenges I have overcome, and the process of doing so, to encourage me in my ability to deal with the current situation.

4. Share my concerns with someone close to me (usually my wife), so we can walk through the challenges together and be stronger as we come out on the other side.

The key question we all must answer when faced with difficult situations—and life will ultimately present us with several of them—is, "How do I respond?" You can choose to feel victimized and unfairly treated, or you can choose to double your efforts to do the very best you can to do the right thing and have an optimistic outlook for the future. We can't choose our circumstances, but we can choose the attitude with which we face them.

Examples from the business side of life, which I hear about frequently, are the issues of compensation and advancement. It seems that all of us feel, at times, that we should be paid more than we are—this is normal. The more challenging situ-

If you spend your life comparing your circumstances to others, you will rarely be satisfied.

ation to manage is when you feel that someone else is *unfairly* paid more than you, or is unfairly promoted ahead of you.

From my experience, if you spend your life comparing your circumstances to others, you will rarely be satisfied. There will always be someone who is better paid, advances more quickly, or gets more recognition than you do. Sometimes it is because they deserve it, and other times it is for other reasons—and sometimes these other reasons don't seem fair. However, if you choose to spend your energy on comparative happiness, you will be miserable.

The right focus is to commit our efforts to earn the recognition we seek, and ask for feedback from relevant people about what we can do to improve. If our conversations with our managers are focused on how we can improve our own performance, instead of comparing ourselves to others, we will be much happier, and will achieve better long-term performance in the workplace.

Adopting a positive outlook allows you to use negative occurrences as learning experiences that offer an opportunity to improve yourself. In this way, each negative circumstance will become another stepping stone to a better, more positive approach to a happy and fulfilled life—a life with as few regrets as possible.

A subtle, but related, topic to the discussion above is the importance of relationships and connections in achieving our goals. Of course, we would like to believe that we operate in a true meritocracy, and will be appropriately rewarded for our progress and contributions in all circumstances. However, that presupposes that the people making the decisions about our future are completely rational and unaffected by relationships and emotions. We certainly know enough from our own life to realize that this is not accurate.

In response to the reality that decisions about our future, compensation, opportunities, and access are often made with a healthy dose of emotion with respect to how the decision maker feels about us, we should thoughtfully pursue relationships with key decision makers in our lives. These relationships not only will open doors for us, but also will provide us with a decided advantage when competing with others for key opportunities.

This is true in nearly every aspect of life (e.g., competing for a business opportunity, trying to get a reservation at a popular restaurant, seeking a promotion at work, getting your children into a coveted school, and many, many others). Take the time to go out of your way to develop relationships with people around you, spend time listening to them (very few people do this today), and take an interest in their circumstances. You will be richly rewarded not only with enhanced opportunities and access, but also with interesting friendships.

All of us will experience disappointment, loss, illness, and setbacks throughout the course of our lives. Very frequently, these difficult circumstances will occur at the most inopportune times. It isn't possible to address all of the potential challenges that life can throw at us, but suffice it to say that the attitude with which we face them will have a significant impact on how well we are able to get through them.

Get as much support as you possibly can from those close to you when you face life's challenges, and maintain a positive, forward-looking attitude as you work through the current difficulties. Remember the areas of your life that you are thankful for, even in the face of adversity. A spirit of gratitude helps us to navigate the most difficult challenges in a much more successful manner.

Above all, don't give up. Keep doing your very best to move forward, even when the odds seem stacked against you.

Chapter 10
Develop the Spiritual Side of Your Life

In the midst of a culture in the United States that seems to be increasingly turning away from the spiritual dimension of life, this chapter may be the most unpopular and provocative one. However, this book is about a life of personal discovery, and the most important life lessons I have learned along the way. But understanding the spiritual side of life is by far the most important of my "lessons learned."

This chapter is written from my personal experience and is not intended to preach to the reader, or to argue for a certain faith or approach to life. The objective is to share my personal perspective, in hopes that it encourages the reader to seek his/her own spiritual truth and awakening, and in so doing to find the true meaning of life.

Many who have come before us have asked the essential question, "Why are we here?" Or stated another way, "What is my purpose?" In my experience, at the most basic level, there are two primary ways to answer this question:

1. We evolved in a random fashion, over billions of years, from a bunch of inert gases, in a "survival of the fittest" world. There is no specific purpose to our lives, but our goal is to live life to the fullest, with a survival of the fittest approach, and with no specific moral underpinning or set of

rules to live by, other than the reality we create for ourselves, OR

2. We were created by an intelligent being (which for the sake of brevity here I shall refer to as "God," while using the masculine pronoun for reference in the discussion), who created us to know Him, and to be a part of the overall plan for the world He created. This Creator also established certain guidelines for us to live by—such as, what is good, and that we were built for relationships, as opposed to solitary lives—and this Creator desires for us to get to know Him.

The first answer provides limited meaning to life, except that we are to survive, excel, and get as much as we can from it. We may choose to pursue relationships with and help for those who live around us, but this motivation must come from our own decisions about how to live life, because we are operating without an overall plan or purpose.

The second answer places us in the midst of a larger story, which we must strive to understand in a deeper way—to understand the life force involved in creating us, and also to understand the role we, and others around us, can play in the overall story. The second answer leads us on a journey of spiritual discovery, while the first answer leads us to a life that is more self-focused, and has fewer sources of meaning that are greater than ourselves.

In my own life, I found the self-focused life to be empty and unrewarding. I have met a number of people who don't have a spiritual emphasis to their lives who are very committed to helping others, however when asked to articulate why they do this, they typically say something to the effect of, "It just feels right to do this."

The deeper question is, "Why does it feel right? Is there a greater purpose to why we are all here on Earth together?" To be honest, without a spiritual foundation, I found it difficult to reconcile, but again, I am writing this from my personal experience.

So, from the perspective of personal reflection, I concluded that there was a Higher Power involved in creating me, and the world around me, including other human beings, as well as the overall environment in which we exist. Little things still remind me of this. When I see a sunset, or witness the beauty of a waterfall, I realize that these scenes didn't have to be beautiful, they could have been colorless, drab grays and browns, with no beauty to them at all. Instead, they are beautiful for a reason—they were made to be beautiful, for all of us to enjoy.

Why would this Higher Power create us? I believe it is for the pleasure of relationships. God created us to enjoy His overall creation, and most importantly, to have a relationship with Him (and with others around us). Ultimately, the goal is that our relationship with God will deepen as our lives move forward, and in so doing, we will gain a more fulsome understanding of our role and purpose here on earth.

Just as I have experienced the incredible joy and fulfillment that comes from establishing deep, meaningful relationships with my family, friends, and co-workers over the years, I have experienced even a deeper and more meaningful joy from deepening my relationship with my Creator since I discovered the importance of this spiritual component to life.

This is the essence of pursuing a spiritual element to my life. I believe there is a force out there that is much bigger, more powerful, and more intelligent than I am, and that this

This emphasis on serving and building relationships with others provides a much deeper and more significant meaning to life than just getting everything we can out of it for ourselves.

force has the capacity to develop a relationship with me, which brings much greater meaning and understanding to my life. Many of the world's religions refer to this force or being as God (in one name or another) and enumerate ways in which we can get to know this God.

There are many different paths described by which we can get to know God. Some religions advocate a monastic existence with a separation from society and a focus on meditation. Others emphasize certain deeds that must be done to earn favor with God, and in so doing to bring us closer to God. Still others advocate more extreme methods of obtaining favor with God.

However, the objective of most religions is somewhat similar, which is for man to develop a deeper, ongoing relationship with God. This accords more meaning to life here on earth, and challenges us to think beyond ourselves to participate in a greater story. This greater story also challenges us to become involved in the lives of others around us, to help them, and improve their lives, out of service to the God who created all of us. This emphasis on serving and building relationships with others provides a much deeper and more significant meaning to life than just getting everything we can out of it for ourselves. This greater meaning comes from developing the spiritual side of our lives, which I believe enriches our life to a much greater degree than anything else we can invest our time in.

As mentioned earlier, I believe that life is all about relationships. Ultimately, I believe the reason for this is that God created us for relationships, both with the people around us and, most importantly, for an ongoing relationship with God.

Of course, the crucial question is, "If this is what we were created for, how do we develop this personal relationship with the God who created us?" I will leave that to each reader to pursue and research on their own, but, suffice it to say, that there are volumes and volumes of ideas out there available for your perusal.

The most important message I will emphasize is to take the time to pursue a spiritual element to your life, look for a deeper truth that extends beyond yourself. Make the commitment to invest the time and energy to develop the spiritual aspect of your life, regardless of the path you elect to pursue. Spend the time to explore your purpose here on earth, and to reflect on the larger world around you, and how you fit into this complicated and exciting world. You will be much better off for doing so.

Remember that life is a journey, and we are to enjoy our journey, learn from it, and continually improve ourselves each and every day of our journey. May you enjoy your journey, and may the ideas and suggestions in this book be of some assistance and encouragement to you along the way.

Appendix
The Archstone Story

When my team and I were asked to assume responsibility for the company that was Archstone's predecessor entity, Property Trust of America ("PTR"), it was late 1994, and PTR was well-liked by investors for its emphasis on owning apartments in moderate income areas in smaller cities in the Southwest U.S. At the time, PTR was the largest owner of apartments in San Antonio and El Paso, Texas, and also owned apartments in Tucson, Arizona and Santa Fe and Albuquerque, New Mexico. The company's mantra was to, "stay out of the way of institutional capital," which tended to concentrate on the large U.S. cities (e.g., Los Angeles, San Francisco, and others).

Being asked to assume responsibility for a well-regarded company, from a highly respected management team is an intimidating task. My team and I set out to conduct a thorough review of the PTR strategy, and come back with our recommendations to the board of trustees for the course we would chart for the future of the company.

After several months of research, we presented our recommendations—the most important of which was that we believed the greatest long-term value in real estate is created by owning outstanding locations in markets where there is very limited land on which to build competitive new product. Interestingly, we believed that this conclusion applied to any type of real estate, whether it was office buildings, shopping centers, hotels, single-family houses, or our product, rental apartments.

This point is most easily illustrated by looking at homes along a popular beach in a market like California, Hawaii, or even Long Island. What you will notice is that the homes located right on the beach front are dramatically more expensive than those that are not on the beach, even if they are only across the street. In fact, homes on the beach can be as much as 10 to 20 times more expensive than homes in the same neighborhood, but not on the beach, even though they are of similar size.

The reason for this discrepancy is simple: The majority of the value of great real estate locations is derived from the value of the land. Therefore, the way to make the most money in real estate, as a long-term investor, is to own property located on the very best land, preferably in locations where there is very little land available on which to build.

Another example of this would be in midtown Manhattan, where virtually all of the land has already been built upon, and you need to tear down an existing structure in order to free up land on which to build new product. The result? Land in great locations in Manhattan is extremely expensive. For apartments in Manhattan, the increases that have occurred in rent levels over past decades are truly extraordinary, creating incredible wealth for those investors fortunate enough to have owned these great locations for the longer term.

Our audacious vision for PTR was that these were the types of apartments (midtown Manhattan) that we wanted the company eventually to own—which was a very long way, indeed, from $300/month apartments constructed of concrete block with cement floors in suburban El Paso, which was the core of our existing portfolio in 1994. Amazingly, in fewer than seven short years from the commencement of our tenure with the company, we would purchase our first high-rise apartment building in midtown Manhattan. In only 10 years we became the largest publicly traded owner of high-rise apartments in New York City—quite a transformation.

Needless to say, when we presented our initial strategy to the PTR Board of Trustees, we didn't recommend selling our apartments in El Paso and immediately purchasing high-rise buildings in Manhattan. This juxtaposition would have been too much of a shock, and in all likelihood, nobody would have believed it was possible.

Instead, we presented an incremental strategy, aimed at moving our capital from what we referred to as "low barrier to entry, commodity" markets, to those which had "high barriers to entry," meaning limited land on which to build new housing, and difficult zoning laws.

The board liked our plan, and the compelling evidence we presented to support our strategy, but was understandably cautious as to whether we would be able to successfully implement our strategy of establishing a large presence in markets in which we had no current ownership. Accordingly, they provided approval in measured increments, allowing us to begin purchasing a limited number of apartments in these locations, as early as 1995. Interestingly enough, 20 years later, the buildings we purchased in coastal California are currently worth seven to 10 times what we paid for them in 1995, underscoring the amazing wealth that can be created from the long-term ownership of exceptionally well-located real estate.

PTR had a sister company called Security Capital Pacific ("Pacific"), which was majority owned by PTR's largest shareholder, Security Capital Group ("SCG"), which our team was also responsible for, and was focused on apartments in California, Nevada, Utah, Oregon, and Washington. Since those were the markets that had characteristics more in line with our long-term goals, it made sense to merge Pacific into PTR and eliminate the duplication of effort. This transaction was completed in mid-1995 and provided our team with the entire western United States in which to operate and invest.

SCG also had another company in which it was the largest shareholder, called, Security Capital Atlantic ("Atlantic"). It was taken public in 1995, and was focused on apartment ownership in the eastern United States.

PTR and Atlantic pursued very different strategies in their respective geographies, with Atlantic pursuing the moderate income strategy in smaller cities (e.g., Raleigh, Memphis, Nashville, Charlotte, etc.) and PTR pursuing a higher income strategy in larger cities (e.g., San Diego, Los Angeles, San Francisco Bay Area, etc.).

Ultimately, as the largest shareholder in both companies, SCG felt it was best to combine the two and create a national apartment platform focused on a single strategy—a transaction that we completed in 1998.

This transaction not only provided us with a national platform, but also gave us a chance to step back and carefully articulate our plans and strategy for the company going forward. As part of our plan, we thoroughly researched a branding strategy for apartments, which we felt could be very successful long term, based on exceptional service. As a catalyst to launch this national branding effort, we renamed the combined company, Archstone, when the transaction closed in 1998.

We also articulated the foundational elements of our strategy and approach to the business:

1. Culture not only matters, but is a key differentiating factor among companies.

2. Values are the foundational element upon which culture is built.

3. Investing in "high barrier" protected markets is essential to creating long-term value for shareholders.

4. Technological innovation offers a key source of competitive advantage.

5. Be true to our word in everything we say and do.

I'm proud to say that these foundational elements were identical over 15 years later, when Archstone was sold in February 2013, and they produced tremendous financial rewards for our shareholders, as well as loyalty and satisfaction for our associates and customers.

Although we were very excited about the merger of Atlantic and Pacific, many of our shareholders were not. They had grown to be very supportive of our protected markets strategy (focusing our investments on markets with very limited land on which to build new housing), and felt we were diluting that strategy by acquiring a portfolio of assets that wasn't representative of this approach to our business. While that was true, what they missed was that the merger was an opportunity to nearly double the size of our company, without the need to raise incremental equity in the public markets, and provided us with the ability to acquire Atlantic's assets at an overall price that was less than what they would sell for in the private marketplace.

In addition, we could thoughtfully monetize these assets over time, allowing us to move the capital into our targeted markets and assets in a disciplined manner, creating significant incremental value in the process.

Almost immediately after closing we began the process of selling all of the assets in markets like Memphis, Nashville, Greenville, and a host of others, and moving the capital to great locations in the Washington, D.C. metropolitan area, as well as Miami, and Boston.

I should also add that in addition to the new markets this transaction exposed us to, the size of the combination (we were nearly $5 billion in total capitalization now) exposed me to all new realms of media and visibility (definitely not by my choice, but visibility to investors is one of the many responsibilities of the CEO of a publicly traded company).

I had never been on live television before, and my first interview came in the context of the announcement of the merger of the two companies, well before the closing. I can tell you that most live television interviews are not what you picture them to be. Instead of being in a comfortable studio, looking at your interviewer, relaxing in a cushy chair, you are sitting on a bar height chair, looking at a camera lens, with no other human being in the room—all the while listening to your interviewer through an earpiece (uncomfortably perched in your right ear) and trying to look relaxed and "natural." Needless to say, I looked neither relaxed nor natural during my first television interview.

I didn't like the live interview format, because I was always worried about what *gotcha* question the interviewer would ask me next. They had lots of time to research and prepare their questions, but I couldn't prepare for all possible questions, and if they asked me something I wasn't ready for, I might look unprepared, or even silly.

It was only after enduring a few of these uncomfortable encounters that a media professional gave me the best advice I ever received for dealing with the media: Treat every live television interview as a free commercial for whatever points you want to convey, regardless of the questions.

The reasoning for this is actually relatively simple. The interviewer looks rude if they cut you off when you are discussing an important concept, so you can continue to articulate your points, as long as you are polite, thoughtful, and genuine, always smiling in the process.

What about if you are asked a question you don't want to answer? Simply employ the concept called "bridging," which involves looking straight at the camera, smiling, and saying, "That is an excellent question, let me tell you about the great things we are doing at our company," and move on to the points you want to make. If the interviewer asks you the same question again, employ the same tactic. They never seem to ask more than twice, and as many times as I employed this approach, only once did I have an interviewer say to me that I hadn't answered her question. At this point, I smiled again and told her what a great question it was, then gave a very brief answer that tangentially addressed her question and moved on to the other points I wanted to make.

The bridging advice was transformational for me, and from this point forward I actually enjoyed live television interviews, and became a somewhat frequent guest on the business-related daytime television shows.

All of this is to say that after the creation of Archstone in 1998, we were no longer a small, somewhat invisible company. With increasing visibility came increasing responsibility.

With our national footprint in place, we began establishing a strong presence in Washington, D.C., as well as Boston, Massachusetts, and began doing the groundwork to enter New York City. Along the way we systematically sold the assets owned by Atlantic that weren't consistent with our strategy (which was virtually all of the assets they owned at the closing of the merger), realizing values far in excess of what we paid for them. This in turn created strong momentum for our company as we built the first nationally recognized apartment platform in high barrier to entry markets.

After the initial objections to the merger with Atlantic, investors again began to warm up to our story, and we developed a very positive following among key investors in public real estate companies.

One of the strategies we had pursued for several years was to identify other publicly traded apartment companies that would be important strategic fits for us on a long-term basis. The most attractive target of all was the largest publicly traded owner of high-rise apartments in the country, the Charles E. Smith Company. The chairman of the company, Bob Smith, was the son of the founder, and a prominent member of the political and social fabric of Washington, D.C. He was a wonderfully interesting person, and I began the process of meeting with him regularly in an effort to establish a long-term relationship, in the event he ever decided to sell his company.

Fortunately, this relationship-building process paid off, and I received a call in early 2001 regarding Bob Smith's interest in pursuing a merger with a well-run apartment company, as a succession strategy for the leadership of his company. After two months of negotiation and strategic discussions, Archstone was fortunate enough to be selected as the company and leadership team to which Bob Smith and his brother-in-law, Bob Kogod, were willing to entrust their life's work.

This was an incredibly transformational event for our company and leadership team, as we would now own the premier high-rise apartment portfolio in the United States, outside of New York City. The long-term prospects for us were unbelievably positive, but as often happens with public companies, the long term prospects can be obscured by short term impacts on quarterly earnings, and this was certainly the case with this merger transaction. The value of a dollar of cash flow from high-rise buildings in the heart of Washington, D.C., was far greater than the value of a dollar of cash flow from the suburban apartment buildings we currently owned. Although we had made excellent progress transforming our portfolio, we still had a long way to go to achieve the locational excellence of the Charles E. Smith Company (Smith) portfolio.

In addition, our extensive due diligence had revealed that there was substantial upside in the rental rates of the Smith portfolio. At many of these properties, we estimated that we could increase rents as much as 25 to 30 percent, and still be competitive with other properties in these markets (in actuality, we were able to increase the rents even more than our initial estimates, creating tremendous value for our shareholders).

We purchased Smith by issuing our common shares to their shareholders, at a price that was a slight premium to their share price prior to the announcement of the transaction. By our estimates, the merger would dilute (or reduce) our earnings approximately 3 percent in the first year after the closing, but thereafter our earnings would grow much faster than they would have without consummating the transaction.

More importantly, the merger would increase the overall net asset value (NAV) of our shares, because we were essentially trading less valuable properties for more valuable properties, at a premium that was far lower than the difference in values.

Despite all of the incredible benefits we described to be realized from the merger, shareholders reacted very negatively to the announcement, and our share price declined over five percent on the day of the announcement. We fielded a lot of very frustrated phone calls, and saw a lot of highly critical analyst reports get published—all in just a few hours after the announcement. It is at times like these that, as a leader, you really need to exude confidence, and encourage your team that we are doing what we believe is right, what we said we would do, and we will be vindicated over time.

The leading sell side analyst on Wall Street at the time published a highly critical piece titled, "What Kind of Kool-Aid Is Management Drinking?" asking how we could have possibly become so deluded as to agree to this foolish merger. I decided that instead of being argumentative and defensive with him, we would try some humor, so I instructed our team to send him a box of Kool-Aid by overnight delivery, with a note saying, "Drink up and you'll see it like we do!" This gesture was a great ice-breaker that led us into a very productive phone call the next morning. The following week we had a detailed meeting in New York City with him, and were able to get him to understand the opportunity from the merger, as we discussed the details of the transaction with him.

Within 18 months this analyst became one of our most enthusiastic supporters, and he and I remain friends (and also even do some business together), to this day.

There are a couple of lessons to take away from this synopsis of the Smith merger:

1. Calmness and confidence under pressure is an inspirational quality of leadership. When things get tough, everyone looks to the leader for clues of how to respond, and leading with confidence and a smile is more valuable than nearly anything else you can do.

2. When people like you, they will generally give you the benefit of the doubt in times of difficulty, or when you stumble. If people don't like you, they are likely to kick you when you stumble and are down. It is much better to treat everyone around you with kindness and respect, even those who criticize you, or compete with you—not only is this the right thing to do, but it also pays great dividends during challenging times.

The Smith merger closed successfully in 2002, and an excerpt from our annual shareholder letter sums up the outcome very well:

EXCERPT FROM 2002 SHAREHOLDER LETTER:

DOING WHAT'S RIGHT, NOT WHAT'S EASY

At Archstone, we are focused on making the best long-term decisions for our company. I believe that the continual emphasis on quarterly earnings that is so prevalent today in Corporate America only serves to motivate management to optimize short-term profits at the expense of long-term opportunities. Our desire to build a truly great company means that we frequently have to make decisions that are inconsistent with maximizing short-

term performance, and are, therefore, unpopular. When we make these decisions, we will explain the reasons for them, and our expectations for future results. Our merger with Charles E. Smith offers an excellent example of this.

When we announced the merger, we also announced that it would be dilutive to short-term earnings and funds from operations. We were roundly criticized for this. Some pundits even questioned whether we understood our business.

At the same time, we also announced that the Washington, D.C. metropolitan area—where 33 percent of our portfolio is now located—was one of the strongest apartment markets in the country, and would continue to be one of the most resilient during times of economic slowdown. As is often the case, the longer-term benefit was largely ignored at the time, and the focus was placed on the short-term dilution.

Today, just 10 months later, the economy is in recession, and the comparative strength of the Washington, D.C. metropolitan apartment market is obvious. During the fourth quarter of 2001, same store revenues grew 6.5 percent in Archstone's Washington, D.C. communities, compared with an overall national average for publicly traded apartment companies of approximately 1 percent.

Of course, many of our critics said we were lucky. If we continue to do our research, plan carefully, and execute our business strategy consistent with our values, we will continue to be lucky. Of course, we will make mistakes from time to time, but that is part of the process of learning and discovery. It is also part of getting better.

The Smith merger was an incredible catalyst in the complete transformation of our company. It gave us the national platform we needed to expand into all of our desired markets, and gave us the size and scale to initiate a number of seminal changes in our industry.

We implemented the first revenue management system for the apartment industry shortly after the closing of the merger, which worked so well that it has since become a standard in the industry. Shortly thereafter, we launched the first online leasing application in the apartment industry, which also completely changed how business was done in our industry.

In addition to these technological advances, we also were making ground-breaking investments into new markets. We purchased our first high-rise apartment building in New York City in early 2002, and quickly followed that purchase with several more exceptionally well-located apartment buildings in New York City. We began the development process on several great high-rise apartment sites in New York City, downtown Boston, and urban Washington, D.C. While we were pursuing all of this expansion on the East Coast, we were also dramatically expanding our apartment portfolio in outstanding locations on the West Coast.

In just four short years, after enduring seemingly unending criticism regarding the Smith merger, we were lauded by nearly every Wall Street analyst as having the best apartment portfolio in the business and for being the most innovative company in our industry. Our stock price increased dramatically, and everything was going as well as it possibly could.

It was during this time that home prices were also rising dramatically across the country, and real estate prices for all types of assets (e.g., apartments, office buildings, hotels, shopping centers, and other assets) were bid up to levels that were unprecedented.

The frenzy to acquire well-located real estate seemed overdone to me, and I convened a meeting of our senior management team at my home to discuss our collective ideas on how to address the opportunities and challenges arising from this environment. This was a time when financing was so readily available for large transactions that leading private equity firms were looking for increasingly larger deals to pursue. We had become large enough by that time that we would make an excellent prize for one of the big private equity firms—many of which had billions of dollars to spend, and limited options in which to invest the capital.

Our senior team agreed, unanimously, that real estate pricing was at peak levels, and the risk of declines in prices was far greater than the likelihood of price increases in the next few years. We also believed that the economy was overstretched, with multiple sectors of the economy running on what seemed to be very aggressive leverage, and the risk of a downside surprise was significant.

Several large private equity firms had previously contacted us about pursuing a potential purchase of our company, so we asked each of those who had approached us to present us with a detailed offer. In a very short period of time, we received offer letters from three well-qualified parties (all subject to confirmatory due diligence, of course) to purchase our company at a substantial premium to the current share price.

Our board of directors made the thoughtful decision to run what is called a "process" (essentially, an abbreviated auction) and required any of the three bidders, who were interested, to submit a binding, fully financed bid after only 10 days of due diligence (an incredibly short time frame in which to evaluate a $20+ billion company, and to fully finance a bid of that size).

The winner of this process was a partnership of Lehman Brothers (a name that is now infamous) and Tishman Speyer (TSP), a highly regarded New York-based international real estate developer and investor.

The buyers had asked that management remain with the company after the purchase closed, which we agreed to do, on a conceptual basis. None of us ever had employment contracts at Archstone, or its predecessor companies, so we expected the same employee-at-will situation to continue after the closing of the merger. Of course, the reality is that nearly all acquirers make management changes after closing a large company purchase, so we expected this to happen sooner or later. Despite this risk, we were confident that a sale of the company was absolutely the right thing to do for our stakeholders, regardless of how it might affect our future employment.

Together with our board, Chaz Mueller, our CFO, and Carrie Brower, our General Counsel, assumed responsibility for negotiating the details of the merger agreement, which was appropriate, so as to avoid any potential conflicts with a CEO who had been asked to remain in place after the closing. The merger agreement negotiations were finalized on the Thursday before Memorial Day weekend 2007, and our Lead Director called to inform me that the buyers were requiring an additional condition of the merger: Unless I signed a detailed employment contract with the buyers, that would go into effect upon the closing of their purchase of the company, they were unwilling to consummate the transaction.

Since I had never had an employment contract during my career, I didn't even have an employment attorney to turn to for assistance. The contract had to be completed by the end of Memorial Day weekend, so we could announce the transaction before the markets opened on the following Tuesday. It was 4 p.m. on Thursday before the holiday weekend, and I needed to find an attorney. Little did I know that I would only sleep a few short hours between then and next Tuesday night, at 10 p.m.

Working with my board and our investment banking firm, we finally identified a well-qualified employment lawyer, after an exhaustive 24-hour effort, including speaking with many firms who were already precluded from representing me by existing conflicts. With my attorney now in place, the buyers sent their initial draft outline of my employment agreement to me for review late Friday evening. The outline alone was well over 20 pages, and unfortunately, nearly all of the major terms were unacceptable to me. It was a brutal way to start a weekend, knowing that my potential inability to agree to terms on an employment agreement might kill an historic $23+ billion transaction.

Without going into tremendous detail, nearly all of the material terms of the initial proposal were very far apart from my objectives for the agreement between us. Among many others, some of the key differences included the amount and type of compensation, and length of contract term. Generally, when you begin a negotiation at opposite ends of the spectrum on price, terms, and ongoing remuneration, it is quite tough to eventually reach an agreement.

Notwithstanding the substantial differences in our respective positions, and the long hours of negotiation over the holiday weekend, we were able to incrementally close the gaps between our respective positions, and move very slowly forward in these complex negotiations.

We finally reached an agreement on all of the documents, but not quite early enough to have everything signed before the stock market opened for business on Tuesday morning. I remember the feeling in my stomach when I had to call our general counsel and tell her that we were still negotiating the agreement, and she would have to call the New York Stock Exchange and suspend trading of our stock this morning until further notice. It was exciting and nerve-wracking, all at the same time.

Within an hour of the opening of the New York Stock Exchange, we had finally signed all of the documents, and we were ready to release the news. I wanted to be in the office to meet with all of our people in person once the announcement was made public, because the shock and surprise was going to be enormous. We were the leader in our industry, and everyone thought we would be an acquirer, not an acquiree.

Although our associates were shocked, our buyers had authorized our management team to assure our people that they wanted to keep our team and platform in place, as well as to grow and expand the company. We would be a private company, but a very large private company with aggressive growth plans. Our associates were cautiously optimistic, but were so loyal to our company that they made me proud. To a person, they committed to continue our company's outstanding performance through the planned August closing date, and I'm proud to say that they all did as promised.

The reaction of our investors did surprise me. Many of the smartest minds in the industry criticized me, and us, for selling the company too cheaply. This is another example of *standing up and doing what is right, even in the face of criticism.* Our board and senior management team strongly believed that we were doing the right thing for our stakeholders, but it was disheartening to read the many, highly critical analyst reports that were published shortly after our announcement.

Interestingly, in less than two months after our announcement, the same analysts would be writing reports saying that the purchase price for our company was so far above current valuation levels that the buyers would be better off paying the $1.5 billion break-up fee than closing the transaction. Although the closing date was extended by two months, which seemed like an eternity for us at the time, as the financial world was falling apart before our eyes, the buyers did close the transaction on the extended closing date in early October 2007.

Of course, as we all know from history, this was the beginning of the biggest financial crisis in the U.S. since the Great Depression, and the purchase of our company would become an important pressure point in Lehman Brothers' fight for survival. A fight they would ultimately lose, in a very high profile way.

The Tishman Speyer team was designated as the day-to-day managing partner of the company, and began the process of directing our lives as a newly private real estate company shortly after closing. TSP has great people, they are smart, talented, and thoughtful, and our team enjoyed working with them a great deal.

The challenge was that the world around us was falling apart, and we had essentially no access to capital with which to grow our business. To make matters worse, the capital used to purchase the company came from several different sources, including loans from third parties, loans from the three banks financing the overall purchase (Lehman, Bank of America, and Barclays), as well as an equity investment from the same three banks, together with TSP.

The idea was to sell the majority of the equity and term loan components to other investors, and for the three banks and TSP to maintain the ownership and control of Archstone. Nearly all private equity transactions were structured in this manner at the time, and if successful, they were very profitable for all concerned.

Of course, nobody expected the financial world to implode as quickly and as dramatically as it did, and the banks' ability to sell positions in the equity and debt from our transaction disappeared completely, which meant that the three of them ended up essentially owning the entire company themselves, which was not their objective.

Only three months after closing, the banks began to pressure TSP to aggressively sell off our assets and pay down the debt load on the company. Of course, by that time asset pricing had declined so dramatically that the sale of even some of our best assets barely brought in enough capital to make a sale worthwhile.

The next several months witnessed a collapse in the U.S. (and world) financial system that nearly caused a repeat of the Great Depression, and saw Lehman desperately fighting for survival. When they filed for bankruptcy on September 15, 2008, the financial world experienced another level of dramatic upheaval, and our business was essentially brought to a complete halt.

We spent the next eight months in what I refer to as *suspended animation*, unable to do anything but keep our properties as fully rented as possible, and serve our customers in a positive and helpful manner.

My encouragement to our people was, "Come to work each day with a smile on your face, so you can be the positive difference in the lives of others you come in contact with, in the midst of a very challenging overall environment." I'm very proud of our people for the incredible positive impact they had on our customers and each other. They were absolutely fantastic during the entire Great Recession.

Probably the most amazing thing about the entire process is that despite not having any financial incentive plan in place to retain our people, our team stayed together at Archstone. They stayed together throughout all of the uncertainty and turmoil brought about by the Lehman bankruptcy, and the potential failure of our company occasioned by this. During all of this turmoil, they also endured the challenge of nearly constant scrutiny by lenders, consultants, and restructuring advisers. Not only did our team stay together, but from 2007 through the sale of the company in 2013, our team produced the best overall property performance (defined as the growth in our same store net operating income during this period) of any of the publicly traded apartment companies. That is what a strong culture and commitment to team members does—it keeps people together in the midst of adversity, and propels superior performance, despite all odds being stacked against them!

In the months prior to the closing of the sale of our company in 2007, we were the largest publicly traded apartment company in the world, based on equity market capitalization. Our largest competitor was Equity Residential ("EQR"), which was slightly smaller than us, and next in line was Ava-lonBay ("AVB"), which was about 40 percent smaller than us. By early 2012, both companies had grown dramatically, as they had taken advantage of the strong investor interest in real estate, to raise substantial amounts of additional capital through the sale of common stock. By contrast, we had decreased in size as we sold off some of our assets to pay down debt and return capital to our owners.

There was a high profile fight among our three bank owners for the ownership of the company, and Lehman ended up writing a multi-billion dollar check to purchase 100 percent ownership of our company from the other two banks. All of this after back and forth posturing that lasted over 18 months and kept our team in heightened uncertainty throughout the process. The check that Lehman wrote to purchase the remainder of Archstone was reputedly the largest investment ever made by an entity in bankruptcy, and was a bold bet by the Lehman board on the capabilities and integrity of our team at Archstone, which was affirming to all of us.

After Lehman purchased 100 percent of our company, we began the laborious process of preparing for an initial public offering ("IPO") to take Archstone public again, and therefore provide liquidity for the Lehman creditors. We were only a week away from launching our road show for the public offering when the news was announced that Lehman had agreed to a deal to sell Archstone to our two largest competitors (EQR and AVB) at a price Lehman had identified as their target price several months earlier.

To Lehman's credit, they were resolute in holding firm to this pricing, while our performance continued to improve, and we progressed closer and closer to a successful IPO.

Although our two competitors had to stretch to get to Lehman's price, they had two powerful incentives to do so. First, we believed we owned many of the best properties in the business, so the opportunity to buy so many incredibly well-located assets was very compelling. Second, and perhaps most importantly, Archstone was a true leader in the publicly traded apartment market, a standard bearer for the industry, and a formidable competitor. Eliminating your most formidable competitor from the landscape is a powerful motivation for pursuing a transaction, and contributed a substantial incentive for them to reach an agreement with Lehman, prior to Archstone completing a successful IPO.

Once again, I had the challenging task of breaking this news to our people, although this time the news was much tougher to hear. With the sale to TSP/Lehman, the buyers wanted to retain our management team and culture. With the sale to EQR/AVB, the buyers would not be retaining our management team, and would only need our associates at the property level, meaning that nearly all of our most senior associates would need to find new employment.

As tough as the process was, our team shined even brighter than before, nearly all choosing to stay in place and produce excellent performance during the several months between the announcement and the closing of the transaction. Both of the buyers and the chairman of the Lehman board told me what a fantastic job our team did in turning over the properties and details to the new owners. I'm incredibly proud of our team for doing the right thing and helping Lehman to obtain an excellent price for their sale of Archstone, even though it caused substantial upheaval for many of our associates as they pursued new employment opportunities subsequent to the closing of the sale.

I'm pleased to say that I have stayed in touch with many of our former associates, and they have found excellent new positions in the industry, or have started companies of their own. They are all doing well, but to a person, miss the camaraderie and culture we had at Archstone—it truly was a very special place.

ACKNOWLEDGMENTS

ACKNOWLEDGMENTS:

This book would not have been possible without the collective contributions of over 3,000 highly talented colleagues at Archstone, who made my job as CEO enjoyable, rewarding, and wonderful in so many ways. I am thankful for each and every one of you, and wish you incredible success and fulfillment in your lives after Archstone. I would particularly like to thank Chaz Mueller, Dana Hamilton, Dan Amedro, Neil Brown, Lindsay Freeman, Carrie Brower, Ariel Amir, Ash Atwood, Rick Jacobsen, Matt Smith, and Dave Brackett who were all fantastic partners with me at Archstone for so many great years.

ABOUT THE AUTHOR:

Scot Sellers retired as the CEO of Archstone, a Standard and Poor's 500 company, in February 2013, after an executive career spanning over 20 years there, most of which were spent as the company's Chairman and CEO. During his 12 years leading Archstone as a public company, Archstone delivered a total shareholder return of over 720 percent and grew dramatically to become one of the largest publicly traded real estate companies in America. Sellers has been fascinated by human interaction since his childhood and has made this one of the cornerstones of his management style and approach to life. This down-to-earth approach to fulfillment and satisfaction in life is the emphasis of his first book, *Regret-Free Living*.

DELIVERING TRANSFORMATIVE MESSAGES
TO THE WORLD

Visit www.elevatepub.com for our latest offerings.

NO TREES WERE HARMED IN THE MAKING OF THIS BOOK.

OK, so a few did make the ultimate sacrifice.

In order to steward our environment, we are partnered with *Plant With Purpose,* to plant a tree for every tree that paid the price for the printing of this book.

To learn more, visit www.elevatepub.com/about

FEB -- 2017

CPSIA information can be obtained
at www.ICGtesting.com
Printed in the USA
BVOW06s0617300117
474805BV00018B/394/P